IN OLD KALGOORLIE

ROBERT PASCOE • FRANCES THOMSON

WESTERN AUSTRALIAN MUSEUM

1989

Western Australian Museum 1989
Reprinted February 1993

ISBN No.: 0 7309 2503 X

© Text - Robert Pascoe 1989
© Photographs - Museum of the Goldfields and Battye Library, Perth

Design: Sally Watson
Typesetting: Scott Four Colour Print

Printed by Scott Four Colour Print, 40 Short Street, Perth, WA 6000
Published by the Western Australian Museum, Francis Street, Perth, WA 6000

IN OLD KALGOORLIE

CONTENTS

He lies here. See the bush
　　All grey through grief for him;
Hoar scrub — like ashes cast —
　　Sprinkles the valley grim.

The saltbush is his shroud,
　　wide skies his only pall,
And 'in memoriam',
　　A thousand stamp-heads fall.

Gold-lured to death — and yet
　　he would have had it so.
Say mass, sing requiem
　　with the grey bush — and go.

Quietly he has found
　　Here in the Golden West,
The long-sought-for at last,
　　An El Dorado blest.

('Prospect Good', 'His Epitaph',
　　The Leeuwin 1911)

INTRODUCTION: DWYER'S KALGOORLIE

Silent eye-witnesses. There were many like J. J. Dwyer, documenting Australian life at the turn of the century by means of the new improved camera. They were not necessarily successful in commercial terms, and most of their work was mundane, restricted to photographing weddings and other social rituals, following the conventions of contemporary photography. As their photographs were not regarded as artworks, connoisseurs did not collect what they produced, and the value of their creations never rose sufficiently for their descendants to bother saving them.

Their customers wanted a precise record of family life, and then complained if the likenesses were unflattering. The public believed the camera caught reality just as it was, ignoring the vast difference between the stereoscopic vision of humans and the monocular, unblinking eye of the camera. Accidental juxtapositions captured by the camera titillated many viewers, but whenever the photographer sought such ironies in his own compositions the artifice seemed too awkward for popular tastes.

Some of these early photographers earned a national reputation in their lifetime: One such was Harry Phillips, the strongly spritual publicist of the Blue Mountains. Nineteenth century photographers such as Antoine Fauchery, Richard Daintree, Henry Beau Merlin, Charles Nettleton, J. W.

Lindt and John Beattie have been properly documented; and early twentieth century photographers whose work has received due attention include Frank Hurley and Harold Casneaux.

It is now time to resurrect John Dwyer, popularly known as Jack Dwyer, photographer of Kalgoorlie, to assess his significance, and look again through his lens at the goldfields' community of Western Australia.

Jack Dwyer stood over six feet tall, an attractive man, with striking red hair. He was always immaculately dressed, and had a predilection for the cream tussock silk suits and panama hats that suited the goldfields' climate, if not the dusty conditions. (1)

John Joseph Dwyer was born on 24 January 1869 in one of the young mining towns in which he was to spend most of his life. Gaffney's Creek was one of several Victorian towns in which goldmining continued after the spectacular rushes to Ballarat and Bendigo had ended.

Jack was the fourth son of six children born to Michael Dwyer, a Tipperary miner who had followed various rushes, but finally settled down. The Dwyer boys were Ned, Dan, Mick, Jack, Matt and Jim, tall men, all interested in the new-fangled machinery and technology of their time, all eventually destined for Kalgoorlie, and all inspired, by parental stories of poverty in ancestral Ireland, to win a better life for themselves.

Jack Dwyer was only three when education in the Colony of Victoria became 'compulsory, secular and free', and he was educated in one of the new government schools at Gaffney's Creek until the age of fifteen. He then left for the Mount Bischoff tin mines in Tasmania and served as a blacksmith for five years, a period of time which presumably included a formal apprenticeship in that trade.

At about the age of 21 Dwyer became a hobbyist photographer, gradually acquiring a professional level of skill, and finally deciding to make a career of it. He went to work for the photographer J. Bishop Osborne, who had studios in Zeehan and Dundas, and stayed for two years, gaining valuable first-hand experience and personal tuition from Osborne. None of Dwyer's earliest photographs survive and the only clue to this phase of his life is to be found in the close relationship between some of his mature photographs and the style of the contemporary Tasmanian cameraman, Beattie.

In 1892 Dwyer returned to Victoria and worked for four years in diverse jobs, which included spending some time as a travelling photographer; but, as there was no shortage of photographers in the straitened circumstances of the mid-1890s, Dwyer retreated to a more secure occupation, as mining contractor on a mercury mine just outside Jamieson and close to his home town.

Finally, in 1896, Dwyer, along with many other Victorians, joined the latest rush and headed off to the West. This was the year in which the goldfields' train went through all the way to Kalgoorlie, and the isolated mining camp became suddenly accessible to the world.

To amass enough capital to set himself up as a photographer he went prospecting through the north-eastern corner of the Coolgardie field, probably the locale of his well-known and evocative portrait of the prospector. (2) The photograph recalls the painterly treatment of a Ballarat digger in Julian Ashton's 'The prospector' (1889), and demonstrates Dwyer's confident use of artistic reference at a reasonably early stage of his photographic career.

At Niagara, now an abandoned township north-east of Kalgoorlie, Dwyer speculated in mining scrip and collected sufficient capital to establish a photographic studio there, but his photographic work had to be supplemented with income as a blacksmith once again.

The only certain route to full-time camera work was in one of the big goldfields' towns, and the following year, at the age of 30, Dwyer won his first opportunity — as special photographer for the Coolgardie-based *Goldfields Courier*. At the time the Old Camp was still the hub of the Western Australian goldfields, a position it was gradually losing to nearby Kalgoorlie. In 1900 he made the big move to Kalgoorlie and a studio of his own. (3) He joined in a partnership with E. C. Joshua, becoming the eighth photographer of Kalgoorlie-Boulder just as the area began to boom.

Dwyer maintained his interest in mining and, through astute investments, laid the foundation of a healthy personal fortune that was to be strengthened by his flourishing photographic business. His first studio was in Hannan Street, the main thoroughfare, but in 1903 he moved across the road to the newly completed Park Buildings, setting up his studio in rooms specifically designed for the purpose. The studio was in the middle of town, alongside the Palace Hotel, and boasted a glass wall and roof to allow daylight in for indoor work, and dressingrooms where patrons could change into their costumes.

He had the latest in cameras, and the most up-do-date props and scenery, essential for creating illusion. He lived at the rear of the premises, and the business consumed his life for the next 14 years.

Dwyer worked in the glass plate era. Negatives were gelatine-coated glass plates that came in two sizes and were known as dry plates because of their processing. The earlier, wet-plate developing process had been more complicated: plates had to be processed within half an hour of exposure, making it necessary for travelling photographers to carry darkrooms with them. The dry plate, an American improvement, was rapidly adopted in Australia after its introduction in America in 1879 when George Eastman patented a machine for making dry plates. However, taking field photographs still remained an arduous undertaking. To capture vistas of the Golden Mile, Dwyer had to cart cameras, tripod and cases of glass plates over mullock heaps and around numereous mine shafts.

Developing was itself a fairly straightforward process, although occasionally, in the hands of inexperienced assistants, disasters could occur. The gelatine plates were set in what was often, because of the climate, hot water, and if handled incorrectly, the gelatine could run and distort the image. A photograph of a group outside the Kalgoorlie Post Office, taken on Federation referendum day, was so distorted as to render the composition hardly recognisable. Dwyer sent the print off to the *Western Argus* and it appeared with a wry caption. A deliberately distorted image of the Goldfields Express was to gain even greater exposure (4). Throughout his career Dwyer continued to experiment and, recognising the value of publicity, to exploit every opportunity. Soon after his studio was established, a local paper boosted his efforts.:

> *A very large photograph of Hannan Street taken from the balcony of the Palace Hotel about 9 pm last Saturday is now on view at Dwyer's studio. A better photograph has probably never been shown in the State. There are some excellent night portraits on view equal, if not superior, to daylight work.*[1]

Studio portraits, a mundane but vital aspect of his craft, formed the bulk of Dwyer's work, and his studio remained open from 7 to 9 pm to take

---

[1] *"Kalgoorlie Miner"* March 1903

advantage of the potential customers drawn to the town centre for evening entertainment.

His clients remember being charmed by Dwyer. A visit to his studio could take twenty years off one's age, as he employed retouchers, generally women with a delicate touch, who removed blemishes and wrinkles from the portrait but left 'character lines' in. A stock of make-up was on hand for visitors to use, including a bottle of red gloss which was liberally applied to their faces. This may have been designed more for entertainment than aesthetic purposes, as the film at that time was monochromatic and, as such, insensitive to red.

An important part of Dwyer's field photography came from mining company commissions from managers eager to record progress for themselves, or photographs to be sent to company directors in London and Melbourne. Favourite subjects included the arrival and installation of new machinery, or visits to the mine by VIPs. Underground shots were lit by magnesium flares, an often unpredictable and sometimes dangerous light source.

For a person steeped in the European tradition of aesthetics, the Kalgoorlie landscape may have appeared stark and uninteresting; yet, it had an attraction for Dwyer, and he photographed both the bush and natural features surrounding the town. He was also an experimental photographer, both in the studio and out of doors, capturing dust storms, lightning and other natural phenomena.

At the time there was also considerable interest in documenting indigenous people. In Australia, papers read at meetings of the scientific community urged listeners to document 'the passing of the Aborigine' and the expedition of Baldwin Spencer and Gillen to the Northern Territory in 1901 aroused considerable curiosity. As a man of his times Dwyer made his contribution, taking many shots of Aboriginal people, in his studio and in their own setting.

Dwyer was a prolific photographer who appeared to delight in his occupation, exploiting every available commercial avenue. His photographs appeared in the *Kalgoorlie Weekly*, and the *Western Argus*, he entered competitions, and he had a selection of his photographs published as postcards.

Dwyer's quickly became the premier studio in Kalgoorlie and at one time he had a staff of 14, but in the years immediately before he left Kalgoorlie

he let the business run down. Other interests and commitments claimed his time, and his health began to fail. From 1915 to 1917 he served on the Kalgoorlie Municipal Council, and was a director of the Kalgoorlie Brewing and Ice Company.

When T. F. Mackay, 'a smart little Scot', was relieving temporarily at the Rembrandt Studios in Boulder, he was approached by Dwyer seeking a purchaser for his studio. Mackay took the studio over in 1917, inheriting the one remaining member of staff, and stayed in Kalgoorlie until 1945. (5) He took some of the equipment to Perth and, in 1971, sold his enlarger and studio camera to the WA Museum, where they were exhibited in 1976 in the newly restored Old Gaol. From 1989 they will be periodically on display in Kalgoorlie's new Museum of the Goldfields.

The studio passed to Fremantle photographer Stuart Gore, who thus inherited an intact collection of late Victorian tricks of the trade which by now seemed antique. In 1948 Gore sold the business to E. Morgan, who eventually closed the studio in 1962.

At 48, Dwyer moved to Perth and established a studio in Hay Street, apparently more as a hobby than a serious business concern. He suffered from headaches and, shortly afterwards, accompanied his brother Dan (who had Parkinson's Disease) to health farms in America in 1918.

The trip may also have been prompted by an unfortunate event which took place shortly after he arrived in Perth. Dwyer became enamoured of a much younger woman; they became engaged, but she broke it off. As he was unable to stay away from her, the affair ended in the Criminal Court, where Dwyer was advised to desist from his attentions. Aired in the gossip columns of the *Sunday Times*, this was the only piece of scandal ever associated with his life.

Dwyer was a keen astronomer. In 1922 he accompanied the Californian Lick Observatory expedition to Wallal on the north west coast of Western Australia to photograph the solar eclipse, with the intention of gathering data in support of Einstein's theory of relativity. Dwyer went at his own expense as part of the Western Australian contingent and assisted with the photography.

Although a wealthy man to the end of his life, Dwyer insisted on cutting his own hair and mending his own boots, and it was such miserly habits, instilled in him by his own parents, that in later years earned him the label of eccentric.

In 1927 he left Australia on a world trip, snapping tourist attractions, fellow shipmates and the moonlight reflected on the ocean. By this time his cumbersome glass plate camera had been replaced by the Box Brownie of the late 1920s. It was the end of an era.

Soon after his return to Perth in 1928 his health failed again, and he died in hospital at the age of 59 on 20 December 1928.[2]

The remnants of his collection of glass plate negatives were destined for the rubbish heap before salvage (decades later) by the local museum, with the assistance of Ken Rout and Peter Englebrecht; and in 1970, 42 years after Dwyer's death, a niece in Perth revealed a previously undisclosed cache.

Jack Dwyer assembled the biggest and best collection of goldfields' photographs in existence. He copied all the important vignettes of the early days, and was present at significant events like Frederic Vosper's speech (6) to striking Woodline workers and Father Long's ingenuous speech from the balcony of Donnellan's Hotel from where he announced to between 4000 and 6000 gold-seekers that a magnificent lump of alluvial gold had been discovered near a salt lake on the Kurnalpi Road. (As the frustrated diggers were to discover, Father Long had been hoaxed and the 'Sacred Nugget' was a piece of iron daubed with gold paint.). His caricature shows him as others remembered Dwyer: the attractive, serious, slightly effeminate professional. (7) He had an intensity of purpose that encouraged people to trust his work, and he seemed to have received enough commissions to live comfortably all those years in Kalgoorlie. Not much is known of the commissions charged by studio photographers, but until the advent of the Box Brownie in the 1920s, they served most people's needs. Dwyer also had his mining investments to fall back on in later life. Towards the close of this life he portrayed himself as the self-assured adventurer in citified 'outback' attire . . . (8)

Photographs from the Golden Mile Museum collection dated before 1898 are copies made by Dwyer, while those after 1917 were taken by his successor, T. F. Mackay. Dwyer's photographs (taken by himself, copied from others, or taken by his assistants and successors) are valuable not only for what they tell us about Dwyer and the history of Australian photograph, but also as a window into the world of Old Kalgoorlie and the Goldfields, from the 1890s to the 1930s.

---

2 Details of Dwyer's life come from various sources, including J. S. Battye, *Cyclopedia of Western Australia* (2 vols, Adelaide, 1912 and 1913) p.898. On the history of photography generally, see David Moore and Rodney Hall, *Australia: Image of a Nation, 1850-1950* (Collins, Sydney, 1983); Derrick I. Stone, *Gold Diggers and Diggings: A Photographic Study of Gold in Australia, 1854-1920* (Lansdowne, Melbourne, 1974).

Young man Dwyer, Kalgoorlie photographer, c1898

Dwyer's famous photograph of the prospector, c1896

The interior of Dwyer's Hannan Street studio, 1908

The freak photograph of the Goldfields Express

T.F. Mackay copying Dwyer's famous Kanowna photograph c1920

A crowd gathers around the great goldfields orator, F. C. B. Vosper

Caricature of Dwyer

John Joseph Dwyer in later life c1928

14

9. Team of prospectors, 1895 (Copy by MacKay 1925) (GMM 1835)

10. Three rabbiters, 1904 (GMM 1082)

11. Alf Kyle's Lease 25-mile, 1895. L to R: (standing) E. Theile; (kneeling) C. Masen; (standing) C. Brown; (kneeling) Col. Cameron; (standing) Jerome de Jaries and Alf Kyle.

12 Studio portrait of the Kalgoorlie Caledonian Society, 1919 (GMM 1164)

13. Young men at Kalgoorlie's first baths, March 1917 (GMM 1533)

14. Mascot in Boulder Fire Brigade fancy dress (GMM 2018)

15. Three elegant women pose for a studio portrait, 1910 (GMM 2806)

16. Using the dryer at a hairdressing salon, 1919 (GMM 1474)

17. Miss A. Farrar, 27 July 1908 (GMM 1196)

18. Annie Throssel and the local branch of the Women's Christian Temperance Union, 1910 (GMM 1191)

19. Women and children at afternoon tea 1923 (Copy by MacKay) (GMM 2115)

20. Women dressed up in Johnny Walker Scotch Whisky costumes 1919 (Copy by MacKay) (GMM 1135)

21. Nuns at St John of God Hospital, May 1910 (GMM 1262)

22. Woman kissing cockatoo, 1907 (GMM 1535)

23. Victoria Park fountain and rotunda, Kalgoorlie 1910 (GMM 1411)

24. Hurley wedding portrait, February 1907 (GMM 1221)

25. Cucel wedding breakfast, Kalgoorlie, 29 June 1910 (GMM 1345)

26. Grange family in their new house 1923 (Copy by MacKay) (GMM 1124)

27. A miner's house, a companion, and a performing dog (GMM 2128)

28. A family portrait, c.1895 (GMM 1296)

29. Charlie, Jessie and Jack Wilson aboard their camel, 1905 (GMM 1002)

30. A Kalgoorlie family and the father's bicycle (GMM 2126)

31. The Hannan Street draper Michael O'Reilly takes his family out in their 1905 Oldsmobile Model C, March 1907 (GMM 1395)

32. D. McKellar and the Kanowna Caledonian Society, August 1907 (GMM 1106)

33. The Irish stall at the local fair (GMM 2098)

A female visitor to the goldfields noticed the obvious:

The first thing that struck me in Coolgardie was, what a splendid lot of men there are here! They were indeed unusually tall, stalwart and good-looking. And why not? The pick of Australian colonies, the flower of our manhood, were here seeking for gold.[1]

At the start it was a masculine world. Gold had been discovered near Kalgoorlie just a few years before Dwyer arrived, and the studio he established became a repository of good photographic documents — taken or copied by him or his successors. **(9)**

The newcomers left their mark on the region, and the countryside was all too often rapidly depleted of the hardy trees that once dominated the landscape. Tree branches were used to construct bough sheds, which offered shade in this harsh environment, and this defoliation only exacerbated the dustiness of local winds. There were no regulations to prohibit the clearing of land close to settlements, although some towns, such as Bulong, kept a one-mile radius of the original salmon runs around them. Men's faces and hands were coarsened by their work in this environment and hats were essential. In 1895, instant chimneys provided creature comfort and mascot dogs were a bachelor's solace.

The tools of fossicking were few and easily portable. Good axes, hammers and digging equipment were prized. Rabbits and the occasional goanna were slung from the belt, having been either trapped in the bush or hunted by well-trained dogs. **(10)** Huts replaced canvas tents only slowly, and a variety of timber, hessian and stone was used to construct such abodes.

Men like the rabbiters came from all parts of Australia, (especially the depressed eastern colonies) to search for the 'yellow boy'. Marvellous Melbourne had gone bust in the early 1890s, with the result that at one

---

[1] May Vivienne, *Travels in Western Australia* (Heinemann, London, 1902).

stage Victorians easily outnumbered the 'Sandgropers' throughout Kalgoorlie and all Western Australia.

As it was necessary to work in teams, they were all mates together. **(11)** Each party of prospectors raised a 'grub-stake', venture capital with which to buy all the necessities. The food they called 'tinned dog', an evocative expression for what must have been unpleasant rations. It might be months before they found 'colour'. Marching out into what were for Europeans inhospitable and out-of-the-way places, the team set up camp and settled in for the duration, prepared for many hours of work, talk and more work. Prospectors needed to supplement their income, and one old-timer fossicker, Mr Abrahams, turned to carting firewood when he lost both arms in an explosion. **(36)**

Prospecting parties were often bands of men joined by ancestry: Scots maintained their identity through Caledonian Societies and in 1919, Mackay took their portrait with a newly-made goldfields honour roll, posed beneath a picture of the beloved Robbie Burns. **(12)**

Theirs was a society which believed in the 'separate spheres' notion of gender relations, in which women and men occupied different areas of life. Men worked and played together; and women were prevented by male superstition from working in the mines, although those who wanted to visit underground could arrange to do so.

The imbalance of the sexes was significant only in the very early period of Kalgoorlie's history, but the separation of male and female lives continued to be a reality until long after the First World War. In 1917, Dwyer photographed the young men of Kalgoorlie lolling in the autumn sunshine at the public baths, where rules prescribed separate hours for men and women. **(13)**

Dwyer's sentimental image of Kalgoorlie women is typified in the photograph of the girl mascot of the Boulder Fire Brigade, who manages to appear feminine although attired in overtly masculine symbols. **(14)** Fire ladders and a house outline the shape of her lower torso and a male caps sits jauntily atop a pretty face trimmed by a lace collar. The bench on which her left arm drapes is supposedly a lovers' seat, but looks for all the world like a charred victim of a recent fire.

As studio subjects, Kalgoorlie women were presented as objects of masculine interest, certainly, but also as possessing their own culture and lifestyle. **(15)** Led by women such as Jean Beadle, Goldfields women were politically active and progressive, and in 1899 they won the right to vote.

Photographing women in their own private surroundings was somewhat more difficult. Although they have left us with fine images of the racetrack and Hannan Street, the male photographers never achieved sufficient intimacy to capture women in their own habitats. The closest they came was through vignettes of women at work, as in the view of the interior of a hairdresser's shop. Here the interest is as much in the mechanical contrivance for drying hair as in the women themselves. **(16)** Kalgoorlie women prided themselves on the quality of their hairdressers, and also on the social function provided by these salons as places where rich and poor could meet, and matrons and prostitutes mingle. No black looks were cast on women who worked 'the Block', as the area of prostitution was known. Since prostitutes were mainly French, Japanese or from other ethnic groups, they were safely and visibly different.

Local ladies such as Miss Farrar, photographed as a young woman in Dwyer's studio in 1917, faced an uncertain future in Kalgoorlie as many of their male contemporaries would not return from the Great War. **(17)** Opportunities for paid female employment in the Goldfields, never excellent, were now few and declining.

The Women's Christian Temperance Union (WCTU), formed in Perth and Kalgoorlie, envisioned a society where women could no longer be victimised by the twin evils of drink and gambling. **(18)** If married men could only be restrained from these depravities, the financial and emotional situation of women and children would be more secure. The WCTU strove to create a Kalgoorlie where Miss Farrar and her generation would be homebodies but, paradoxically, the WCTU was also successful in educating many women in the finer points of public activism. Their dress was lacily feminine but they showed a preference for muted white and they all wore brooches. The nurse (bottom left hand corner) was an important member of the group; nurses at this time wore their uniforms (without cap and apron) as day dresses to signify their calling at all times. Because the WCTU members were workers, keen to help their fallen sisters, they went gloveless. As ideologues, they had a difficult time of it in Kalgoorlie, as goldfields' society was too hard-bitten and too phlegmatic for temple-builders.

To be a Kalgoorlie woman meant making the best of an imperfect situation, instead of dreaming of a world where life might be easier. At an afternoon tea with other women of the neighbourhood it did not matter that your teacups did not match; a piece of lace could be thrown over a makeshift table, and the cake served quite elegantly. **(19)** The sparkling white blouses of the women photographed sit at odds with their weathered complexions, but the daughter looks fetching in her one good dress, and would amuse herself for hours pulling her stuffed toy dog around the yard in the model train Dad had knocked together.

Female conversation was not idle but concerned with the pressing problems of the day. 'Has anyone seen Mrs Richards since the condensed water wrecked her baby's stomach lining?' . . . 'How on earth do you get your lawn and these vines to grow in this climate' . . . Why do those Italians always walk arm-in-arm and force us to take our prams off the footpaths? At least they don't drink like my Jim . . .'

Alcohol was an important and indispensable part of this culture, part of the British heritage, as suggested by the Georgian clothes worn by mannequins dressed in the manner of Johnny Walker Scotch Whisky (20) There were so many hotels in Hannan Street that a mythical prize supposedly awaited the man who could successfully take a drink in each one and keep walking.

Because drinking, gambling and prostitution were intrinsic to goldfields' society and culture, the moral force of churches was strained, but nuns at the convent school in Coolgardie and at a hospital in Kalgoorlie earned themselves a special position. In a society with few recognised rules and regularities, the world of the nun appeared perfectly symmetrical and well-ordered to Dwyer. (21)

Nurses too were paid enormous respect by the goldfields' men, and nursing was one of the few career occupations open to women. Women who lived alone would excite less gossip here than elsewhere, for many wives, mothers and girlfriends were often left alone for weeks at a time while menfolk wandered in search of work or went prospecting. Widows were numerous in a dangerous industry like mining, and women could live together, sometimes surrounded by a menagerie of animals and a jungle of plants. (22) The sight of a woman kissing a cockatoo may have seemed odd to Dwyer, and therefore worth photographing; coincidentally, a similar snapshot was taken in Gundagai, New South Wales, in about the same period.[2]

About courtship little information survives, but one apocryphal item is important:

Do you ever dream, my sweetheart, of a twilight long ago,
Of a park in old Kalgoorlie, where the bougainvillaeas grow?

asked Herbert Hoover of the local barmaid with whom he became acquainted while working as an engineer in the district. The park would have been Victoria Park, not far from Hoover's Mullingar house, and not too distant from the Hannan Street pubs. As Dwyer's photograph reveals, it was nowhere as lush a park as Hoover remembered it many years later. (23)

Where the moonbeams on the pathways trace a shimmering brocade,
And the overhanging peppers form a lovers' promenade?
Where in soft cascades of cadence from a garden close at hand,
Came the murmurous, mellow music of a sweet, orchestral band.
Years have flown since then, my sweetheart, fleet as orchid blooms in May,
But the hour that fills my dreaming, was it only yesterday? . . .[3]

Hoover was already betrothed to the woman who would become Mrs President, and the reported liaison with the Australian girl was merely symbolic of the casual quality of Kalgoorlie courtships. Men and women had declared a truce in this frontier town where crimes of rape and sexual assault were markedly fewer than elsewhere in Australia, largely as a result of the open brothels. Men who tried to womanize often met their match:

Dr Swanston was a clever surgeon and gynaecologist, and a favourite with both sexes. The only people with whom he wasn't popular, were his professional brethren, and mammas with marriageable daughters. His competitors of the medical faculty would either shrug their shoulders, or slowly wink the other eye, whenever his name was mentioned. His peccadillos were the talk of the town, and when some of these compromising letters were made public, he decided to leave home. His fear of the handsome, black-eyed Jewess, who twice publicly attempted to stab him, on the latter occasion seriously, and the expensive diversion of keeping two homes, was so real that he left suddenly for New Zealand! [4]

---

[2] Peter Quartermaine, *Gundagai Album: Early Photographs of an Australian Country Town* (National Library of Australia, Camberra. 1975) p. 107.

[3] The Hoover verses were collected by Arthur Reid, who knew him, and have found their way into various anthologies of folksongs. See also Geoffrey Blainey, 'Herbert Hoover's forgotten years', *Business Archives and History* 3 (February 1963) pp.53-70; and A. Heintz, 'Herbert Hoover's forgotten Australian years', *Walkabout* 32 (July 1966) pp.33-35. In 1987 the verses were translated into Italian by Nino Randazzo in his *Le fiamme di Kalgoorlie*.

[4] Arthur Reid, *Those Were The Days* (Perth, 1933) pp. 69-70.

The Cornish attitude to sex was notoriously fey, as revealed by this typical goldfields' limerick:

A demure little maid of Kalgoorlie,
For months had been quite - - - fed up.
so she journeyed to Perth,
To diminish her - - - appetite,
And returned home quite de-lighted.

A cousin from Cornwall named Fregnant,
God wed to hower Mary of Redruth.
Said Mary's papa
When told by - - - Cousin Ann,
A'h deed'n know hower Mary was - - - that way.

The wedding was a serious ritual, worth taking trouble over, despite the primitive conditions and the fact that there were few churches; other aspects of the ritual, such as the breakfast, were also considered well worth recording. **(24)**

J. F. Cucel and Stella Adda Garden took breakfast together on 26 June 1910 at the home of her parents at 47, Lionel Street. Her father asked Dwyer to record the occasion, which proved a difficult assignment. The children would not sit still, the blind had to be drawn to control the quality of light and although the clergyman obligingly shifted sideways, he would not look at the camera. **(25)**

The new couple were inevitably committed to starting married life in a house somewhat less glamorous than those of their metropolitan contemporaries. In their minds, however, it was a distinct improvement on what had been available in the pioneering days of the 1890s.

Mrs C. C. Richards described the first house she lived in when she and her children rejoined her husband at Coolgardie:

Puppa had a 6-by-8 tent and his bunk inside was four forked sticks driven into the ground with two 6 ft poles across them and two oat bags for a mattress. The table was a box turned upside down on four more sticks driven into the ground. What fascinated the children was the big bush shed with table and seats all made with poles in the ground, and boards nailed on for seats.

The hanging safe was a chaff bag; billy-cans and kerosene tins were the cooking utensils. The fireplace, about 6 ft from the shed, was built

round with stones and tins to shelter the flames. In one corner of the shed a box was let into the ground, with a lid on it. That was for the bread and brownie (a cake) which Puppa had made the day before.[5]

That was 1895. Six years later, in 1901, the first Federal census revealed that seven goldfields' houses out of every ten were still built in this makeshift manner. By the mid-1920s living conditions were distinctly better, but even a medical practitioner like Dr Grange expected his wife, baby and sister to live in rough-and-ready surroundings, 1923. **(26)** Apparently the back section of this house served as a ward for his patients. Doctors were not especially wealthy, but they enjoyed trappings such as the buggy and the motor car.

The tradition of ingenious practicality continued even when the standard of housing improved. Houses were designed for easy dismantling and carriage, and additional rooms were added as the need arose.

Only the biggest houses and key social institutions in the main towns were built in brick and stone.

Indeed, the quintessential Kalgoorlie home was the modest miner's house of weatherboard and galvanised iron, built with the principles of bush adaptation and utility in mind. Pepper trees and tamarisks were planted to help shield houses from the heat and dust, and fences kept goats in and dust out. The front verandah was a cool and relaxing spot, and it was also part of street life, close enough to enable the householder to hail passing neighbours from the comfort of an easy chair. **(27)**

When weather permitted the family table could be moved out to the backyard, which had a valuable domestic function. The heavy and dirty work of the laundry and stables belonged here, as did the family's vegetable patch (an important addition to the household income). Children's pets and fowls also battled for a corner. One family, apparently in Kalgoorlie, in 1895 had at least one dog, two bicycles, a perambulator and a dromedary camel dwelling on their property. **(28)**

One form of goldfields' transport at the time was the camel, on to which one could put both the mate and the missus, with room left over for a child. Hundreds of 'Afghans' emigrated to Western Australia from

---

[5] Mrs C. C. Richards, *Memories of a goldfields mother*, JRWAHS 1948, pp.12-16; repr. Marian Aveling, ed., *Westralian Voices* (UWAP, Nedlands, 1979). Other sources on women include Margaret Bull, *White Feather: The Story of Kanowna* (Fremantle Arts Centre Press, 1981) chapter 12.

Afghanistan, Baluchistan, India and Pakistan, bringing with them so many camels that Australia became the world's leading supplier of these animals. The Afghans and the Chinese were prohibited by law from working in mines, so instead they established essential camel transport and laundry businesses in and around Kalgoorlie. Camels required expert handling and were not particularly comfortable. **(29)**

Bicycles were generally preferred. A man could park his bike outside the front gate without fear of theft, and two mates could cycle together for hours to visit a picnic spot on their day off. **(30)** (The standard cure for a puncture halfway between hamlets was plenty of grass stuffed into the pneumatic tube.) The bicycle was probably more important and more intensively used on the Western Australian goldfields than any other rural area of the world in the 1890s.[6] Professional cyclists raced along the bush 'pad' made by camel tracks to deliver the mail in the 1890s. For decades afterwards it was still possible to identify the remnants of these bicycle pads, thin ribbons of hard-surfaced earth snaking their way north, east and south of Coolgardie to outlying settlements. Just wide enough for a bicycle, these pads were a tribute to hardy legs.

As his brother owned a dealership, Dwyer had a personal interest in cars which inspired him to take some original photographs, but the role of the car in pre-war Kalgoorlie was limited. Roads were often impassable to the motor car, the purchase price was very high, and cars were owned only by mining officials, doctors and big storekeepers like Hannan Street draper Michael O'Reilly. **(31)** Trains and trams shuttled miners back and forth to the Golden Mile with great efficiency. Even as late as 1920 there were very few cars in Kalgoorlie, while the streets of Perth and the inner suburbs were crowded with traffic. One goldfields' politician stood up in parliament once every year to ask the same question: "How many pedestrians were killed and injured by cars these last twelve months?" [7]

Different goldfields' areas acquired particular ethnic identities. Boulder was mainly Cornish and Welsh, and South Boulder noticeably Italian and Slav as the 1920s wore on. Scottish and Irish clubs and associations were set up very early, and even a short-lived town like Kanowna had its own Caledonian Society. **(32)** The Irish intermingled easily with other British tribes, but retained their own identity. The northern suburbs of Kalgoorlie, especially Lamington, Piccadilly Heights and Mullingar, were dominated by the English, Scots and wealthier Irish, as well as a sprinkling of educated foreigners. **(33)**

The 'crimson thread of kinship' which linked Kalgoorlie with the United Kingdom was important in determining who should marry whom, the quality of local street life, and the survival of certain institutions. Prostitution as a business was kept alive by influxes of new non-British immigrants. The Irish and English tradition of the pub found ready expression in Kalgoorlie, and Irish, Welsh and other miners dominated trade union life. Masonic lodges, exclusive clubs like Hannans, and sentimental associations such as the Caledonians and the megastar musical groups persisted in Kalgoorlie's subsequent development. An acceptable *modus vivendi* was reached between the mate and 'his' missus, but there were many non-British people excluded from the dominant tribe; and prospecting parties, the cornerstone of mateship, were seldom ethnically mixed.

Team of prospectors, 1895

[6] Jim Fitzpatrick, *The Bicycle and the Bush* (Oxford University Press, Melbourne, 1980).

[7] Rick Grounds, 'The business of urban history: Selling the motor car to Western Australia' (BA Honours Thesis, Murdoch University, 1978).

Three rabbiters, c1904

Alf Kyle's Lease 25-mile, 1895. L to R: (standing) E. Theile; (kneeling) C. Masen; (standing) C. Brown;
(kneeling) Col. Cameron; (standing) Jerome de Jaries and Alf Kyle

Studio portrait of the Kalgoorlie Caledonian Society, 1919

Young men at Kalgoorlie's first baths, March 1917

Mascot in Boulder Fire Brigade fancy dress c1906

Three elegant women pose for a studio portrait, c1910

Using the dryer at a hairdressing salon 1919

Miss A. Farrar, 27 July 1908

Annie Throssel and the local branch of the Women's Christian Temperance Union, 1910

Women and children at afternoon tea 1923

Women dressed up in Johnny Walker Scotch Whisky costumes 1919

Nuns at St John of God Hospital, May 1910

Women kissing cockatoo 1907

Victoria Park fountain and rotunda, Kalgoorlie c1910

Hurley wedding portrait, February 1907

Cucel wedding breakfast, Kalgoorlie, 29 June 1910

Dr Grange and family in their new house 1923

A miner's house, a companion, and a performing dog c1921

The Waller family portrait, c1895

Charlie, Jessie and Jack Wilson aboard their camel, 1905

A Kalgoorlie family and the father's bicycle c1906

The Hannan Street draper Michael O'Reilly takes his family out in their
1905 Oldsmobile Model C, March 1907

D. McKellar and the Kanowna Caledonian Society, August 1907

The Irish stall at the local fair c1906

Exploration party setting off, 1896

34. Exploration party setting off, 1896 (GMM 1333)

35. Digging a costeen at the Victory North gold mine, St Ives (GMM 1628)

36. Armless Abrahams bringing in firewood by goatcart 1906 (GMM 2181)

37. Miners resting under shade at Mt Monger gold mine 1922 (GMM 1280)

38. The proud directors of the Kurrawang Firewood Co."S.A. Premier & Party" train, 1912 (GMM 1282)

39. Mealtime at the boarding house of the Kurrawang woodline, 2 August 1908 (GMM 1334)

40. One of the Coolgardie goldmines, Lord Bob's, showing whip poles and tip-drays, November 1907 (GMM 1033)

41. Moustachioed miners and their mascot, (Copy by MacKay) c1929 (GMM 1727)

42. Paddington Consols battery, 11 July 1908 (GMM 1332)

43. Tributors at Paddington Consols, the same day 11.7.1908 (GMM 1321)

44. Members of the Chamber of Mines assembled in 1908 (GMM 1506)

45. A group of miners about to start their shift, Paddington Consols, 11 July 1908 (GMM 1615)

46. The workforce of the Kalgurli gold mine, 1908 (GMM 2292b)

47. Hidden Secret gold mine, March 1907 (GMM 1426)

48. The Lancashire boilers in the No.1 boiler house of the Golden Horseshoe gold mine, September 1903 (GMM 1027)

49. Carrying in the first zinc boxes, Lake View Consols, 1896 (GMM 1067)

50. Front and back views of the Vajen-Bader Breathing Apparatus, first patented in the USA in 1891, 1910 (GMM 1047)

51. Truckers about to load ore for ascent up the main shaft of Great Boulder gold mine 1903 (GMM 1337)

52. Miners in a drive of the Kalgurli gold mine, October 1903 (GMM 1634)

53. A frameset in use at the Oroya Brownhill gold mine, December 1903 (GMM 1500)

54. Queue of swivel trucks at Perseverance gold mine, September 1907 (GMM 1322)

55. Some of the most important men in Western Australia crowd around the Golden Eagle nugget, discovered on 15 January 1931 by the son of Jim Larcombe pictured here in the dark suit (GMM 1199)

56. A dinner for the staff of the Kalgurli gold mine, 7 November 1907 (GMM 1134)

57. Portrait of Detective P. D. Kavanagh, responsible for protecting the gold from theft 1908 (GMM 1479)

58. Harry Pell and assistant conducting the Hannan's Open Call 1920 (Copy by MacKay) (GMM 1260)

59. Clerical staff at the Western Australian Machinery Corporation office 4.5.09 (GMM 1118)

60. Nurse Egan's hospital c1908 (GMM 2123)

61. Government Hospital operating theatre, 1909 (GMM 1536)

62. The main ward at the Government Hospital, 1909 (GMM 1086)

Prospecting in the goldfields was arduous and chancy. The paradox of mineral exploitation is that prospecting parties are oblivious to everything except what they are looking for. The early explorers knew the general appearance of auriferous country, and trotted off, well-provisioned, in their camelcades. **(34)**

Having identified an area as promising, the next step after loaming was the digging of a costeen (sometimes spelt 'costean'). The reefs in the Kalgoorlie area ran north-south, which generally, but not always, called for east-west costeens: lodes could be convoluted, as around Menzies. **(35)**

As costs rose, company mines took over the goldfields. Officials and backers of the Victory North Gold Mine looked over the shoulder of the labourer as he completed the digging of an exploration trench at St Ives. Since the 1950s geologists have searched for other minerals: nickel was sought in the 1960s and found around Kambalda, just 50 km south of Kalgoorlie.

Besides capital, deep-mining also required quantities of wood to power the new machinery. The men who cut this firewood were almost as numerous as the mining ground staff, and indeed were often out-of-luck prospectors. **(36)** Even in the remotest bush, the headframe, that potent symbol of gold below, made its ubiquitous appearance whenever a company thought there was much of a chance. At Mount Monger the headframe replaced a smaller operation headed by an old windlass. Otherwise known as a 'poppet', the mine's superstructure grew in size above the ground the deeper the shaft sank below ground. **(37)**

Still more wood was needed in the early years of the century. The stocks around Kalgoorlie were rapidly depleted and woodcutters began to move further afield. Entrepreneurs such as W. N. Hedges devised a solution: miles of railway line along which were to run private 'Woodlines'. The most famous of these was the Kurrawang Woodline Train, capable of hauling more than 40 carriages groaning under its load of wood. **(38)** These Woodlines scarred the land indelibly, cutting swathes through the bush. Deforestation contributed to the dust storms that assailed Kalgoorlie from the northwest in the mornings and the south in the evenings. They said you could almost pick the prevailing wind direction from the colour of the dust.

The woodcutters employed in these timber operations lived in rustic conditions. **(39)** They were a militant bunch, and offensive to respectable society in many ways, which included their practice of living with Aboriginal women. The woodliners certainly appeared less respectable than the miners living in isolated hamlets such as Burbanks or Lord Bob's, the southern suburbs of Coolgardie and virtual fiefdoms under the control of the local manager. **(40)**

Most goldminers, and certainly the ones who defined the mystique of this occupation, were employed on one or other of the various company mines in the Golden Mile. They were a tough, individualistic lot whose loyalty to trade unionism or other collectivist impulses was always modified by opportunities to 'strike it rich' themselves. **(41)**

The first miners carried little in the way of safety equipment and thought of themselves as temporary employees.

As gold became harder to win after about 1897, the scale of mining operations grew. Mineworkers at Paddington Consol organized industrial action a few years before a cheerful portrait of the mine's battery was taken in 1908. **(42)**

Mining companies were themselves in straitened circumstances: refractory or sulphide ores were encountered; most of the companies floated were unsuccessful, and the promoters were the only beneficiaries. Australian and British promoters worked hand-in-glove with London brokers to puff and then unload dubious enterprises. Companies on the Golden Mile were fiercely competitive and their refusal to cooperate delayed the introduction of new techniques for winning the ore. Instead they cut labour costs, especially through the growing preference for tributors — mining sub-contractors. Tributors were shrewd and experienced miners who paid an agreed fixed sum to work an area and keep any profits. **(43)**

The industry as a whole was ruled, however, by the hard-boiled engineers and financiers who made up the Chamber of Mines, which had its headquarters in the centre of Kalgoorlie. One such was Richard Hamilton (middle of first row) who was even tougher than the miners: he confronted a crowd of miners single-handed outside the Chamber on one occasion, and on another sent 'scabs' in Red Cross vehicles to break a strike. **(44)**

The workforce of each mine was divided along lines of skill and ethnicity. The men at the rockface considered themselves the elite, and earned more as a consequence of union pressure. **(45)** They were particularly keen to keep out 'foreigners', by which they meant miners of non-British ancestry. Fragmentation among mineworkers prompted a famous ditty 'The Exile' from the pen of a local poet who signed himself or herself 'The Exile':

> *The oilrag is the Labor toff,*
> *he holds the miner dirt,*
> *The trucker wouldn't dare to touch*
> *a miner's dirty shirt,*
> *Then if the mullocker presumes,*
> *the trucker gets annoyed,*
> *And all possess a lofty scorn*
> *for Boulder unemployed.*
> *Supposing, lads, we sling this pride*
> *and try another plan,*
> *And institute a better code,*
> *the Brotherhood of Man.*[1]

Any Golden Mile mine was a large and complex operation which combined the talents of many workers. **(46)**

---

[1] Quoted by Beverley Smith, 'Early Western Australian literature' (MA, University of Western Australia, 1963) part-published in *University Studies on Politics and History*, 5 and 6.

The technology of the above-ground workings remained much the same from the late 1890s until the early 1920s. Alongside the headframe was the winder-house, where the cables going down into the shaft were controlled. Ore was stored in bins or dumped unceremoniously somewhere near the headframe. **(47)** Meanwhile, massive boilers were stoked with firewood to produce the energy for the mine's water pumps, ventilation systems, lighting, winder cables and other requisites. **(48)**

Gold was displaced from solutions in boxes filled with zinc shavings, a task undertaken by unskilled labourers working on the surface. **(49)** Once the ore was taken out of the mine, it had to undergo numerous treatment processes, and the labourers involved in these areas were more directly under the charge of the white-collar workers above ground.

Not so for the underground workers. There were 'shift bosses', but effective supervision of the miners was impossible. The dangers involved and the fear generated by working underground were such that goldminers relied to a great extent on each other, at least on a day-to-day basis. In the event of trouble some fancy equipment was available — such as the Indiana-patented Vajen-Bader Breathing Apparatus for rescuing men overcome by carbon monoxide fumes. **(50)** But men were sceptical of the worth of such equipment and, fairly or not, blamed the companies for inadequate ventilation facilities. They preferred to rely on each other, comforting themselves with success stories of individual heroism, like the extraordinary rescue of Modesto Varischetti, an Italian miner trapped in a flooded mine in 1907.

Much of the problem was indeed psychological. The descent alone was unnerving: the cage plummeted down the shaft at considerable speed, or so it seemed from inside. The newcomer was quickly disoriented in the directionless underground working area, where foreign smells and noises added to his sense of disquiet. The feeling of entombment was compounded by the amount of time it took to get anywhere in a mine: from boarding the 'skip' at ground level to arriving at his workplace might take a man 30 minutes. There was a cage for miners, a 'skip' on one side for the ore, and a ladderway for men to get up or down to the next platform.

Truckers loaded their ore-trolley into the 'skip' and waited at the 'plat' for its return. Each numbered platform was 100 feet below the previous one, and from each one extended hallways cut into or under the seam of gold. **(51)**

A 'drive' ran horizontally; in October 1903 two managers working by candlelight surveyed the outer extremity of such a drive while two machine-miners worked ore loose with a powerful drill attached to a brace. The fumes caused by drilling 'dusted' the men's lungs, earning the drills the epithet 'widow-makers' **(52)**

Truckers were the gossips of the mine. In between the hard work of trundling loads of ore to the shaft they had periods of waiting for the skip, during which they had time to chat among themselves. If there was a problem they were the first to notice it, or spread the word: an unpopular shift boss on the way, an explosion somewhere in the mine, or fisticuffs between two miners. They were the first to know, and their reports influenced what would happen next.

While a drive was horizontal, the 'stope' referred to the excavation of ore dug from below. The 'frameset' was introduced to make this process quicker. If a wide lode was encountered, a carpenter would prepare a set of posts and caps rather than the usual complete walls and ceiling. Waste rubble accumulated behind this 'set' and men could get up by ladder to 'shrink-stope' the ore above. Using the drill in this upright position was extremely taxing. **(53)**

A traffic jam would often occur as the younger men pushed their trucks to the shaft. 'Bendigo trucks' were amongst the most commonly used, with a hinged door at one end and a swivel which enabled the contents to be rapidly emptied in any direction once the trucks had got to the top. **(54)**

Outside the mining enterprise itself there was a wide range of associated occupations: there were speculators and financiers, engineers and managers — such as those at the historic presentation of Jim Larcombe's Golden Eagle nugget. **(55)** Many of these lived in prosperous suburban Mullingar, and quit the goldfields about the same time as Dwyer. Each mine had many white-collar workers, employed as paymasters and engineers. **(56)** To regulate the industry, an army of government officials was needed, including wardens to adjudicate disputes between prospectors or companies, and a special Gold Stealing Squad headed by the redoubtable P. D. Kavanagh. **(57)**

Locals were able to speculate in mining scrip through the medium of Hannan's Open Call. Harry Pell was the son of a University of Sydney mathematics professor and had inherited a quick head for figures. His 'Open Call' became a popular evening recreation for both men and women, and his future wife, Lisha Buscombe, fell in love with him while watching his performance. **(58)** One of their children, Olive Pell, became a Western Australian poet.

The WA Machinery Company was one of a handful of long-running local businesses which provided the specialist machinery necessary for the mines. Its expertise seems to have been mainly in the importation of machinery from Britain and North America rather than in domestic manufacture. The company also did a roaring business acquiring used machinery for the purpose of resale, sometimes accepting a share in the mine as payment. Its business was conducted in a typical office of the early twentieth century, with male clerks perched on stools doing the copperplate work by hand, a female typiste operating the new-fangled typewriters, and a male secretary or supervisor. **(59)**

While this was a new and expanding area for the employment of women they never expected to enter the career structure of the office, as an intelligent copy boy may have done. A popular avenue for the employment of women was nursing **(60)** Nurse Egan's Hospital and the Government Hospital always needed nurses, as mining was dangerous and the effects of a dusted lung might not be apparent for many years. Many Italian miners preferred to go home to die rather than sit it out in Kalgoorlie. The operating equipment was primitive, though comparable to that available in Perth; **(61)** the wards were not cheery, and certainly not well insulated against the goldfield's heat. **(62)** Dr Barber was, according to Arthur Reid, one of the best-known doctors in Kalgoorlie at the time, along with Dr Arkle, Dr MacMillan, and the ill-starred Dr Swanston.

The hospitals were a reminder that goldmining was not a glamorous profession. Cave-ins, explosions and pthisis were real dangers, and although Perth may have had as many orphans as Kalgoorlie, many miners never married nor had children. Teenagers started with fossicking or salvage jobs and then, as young men, they became mullockers, doing the intense labouring jobs above ground. In their mid to late twenties they moved underground, starting as truckers and eventually moving onto the real work at the ore-face. With increased perils, of course, came not only additional pay, but that quality of mateship which, in the poem of Olive Pell, was the real 'gold to win':

What is the search for gold in the ground
never sold
seldom found?
It's the sweat and the fear,
the hunger, the beer
that holds in a dream
gold's sparkle and gleam,
quenching a thirst
dry as cant
as dying plant,
bursting like cyclonic rain
to drown a taste to mope,
giving hope
not strength, to face again
the unrewarding track,
that holds the pick, the spade, the pack,
the dust and flies,
heat faded skies,
the dark confines of the shaft —
and the mate who laughed . . .
This is gold to win.[2]

---

[2] Olive Pell, *Gold to Win* (Hawthorn Press, 1964).

Digging a costeen at the Victory North gold mine, St Ives c1904

Armless Abrahams bringing in the firewood on goatback 1906

Miners resting under shade at Mt Monger gold mine 1922

The proud directors of the Kurrawang firewood train 1912

Mealtime at the boarding house of the Kurrawang woodline, 2 August 1908

One of the Coolgardie goldmines, Lord Bob's, showing whip poles and tip-drays, November 1907

Moustachioed miners and their mascot, 1895

Paddington Consols battery, 11 July 1908

Tributors at Paddington Consols, the same day 11.7.1908

Members of the Chamber of Mines assembled in 1908

A group of miners about to start their shift, Paddington Consols, 11 July 1908

The entire workforce of the Kalgurli gold mine, c1908

Hidden Secret gold mine, March 1907

The Lancashire boilers in the No. 1 boiler house of the Golden Horseshoe gold mine, September 1903

Carrying in the first zinc boxes, Lake View Consols, 1896

Front and back views of the Vajen-Bader Breathing Apparatus, first patented in the USA in 1891, 1910

Truckers about to load ore for ascent up the main shaft of Great Boulder gold mine c1903

Managers and miners in a drive of the Kalgurli gold mine, Oct 1903

A frameset in use at the Oroya Brownhill gold mine, December 1903

Queue of swivel trucks at Perseverance gold mine, September 1907

Some of the most important men in Western Australia crowd around the Golden Eagle nugget, discovered on 15 January 1931 by the son of Jim Larcombe pictured here in the dark suit

69

A dinner for the staff of the Kalgurli gold mine, 7 November 1907

Portrait of Detective P.D. Kavanagh, responsible for protecting the gold from theft c1908

Harry Pell and assistant conducting the Hannan's Open Call 1920

Clerical staff at the Western Australian Machinery Corporation office 4.5.09

Nurse Egan's hospital c1908

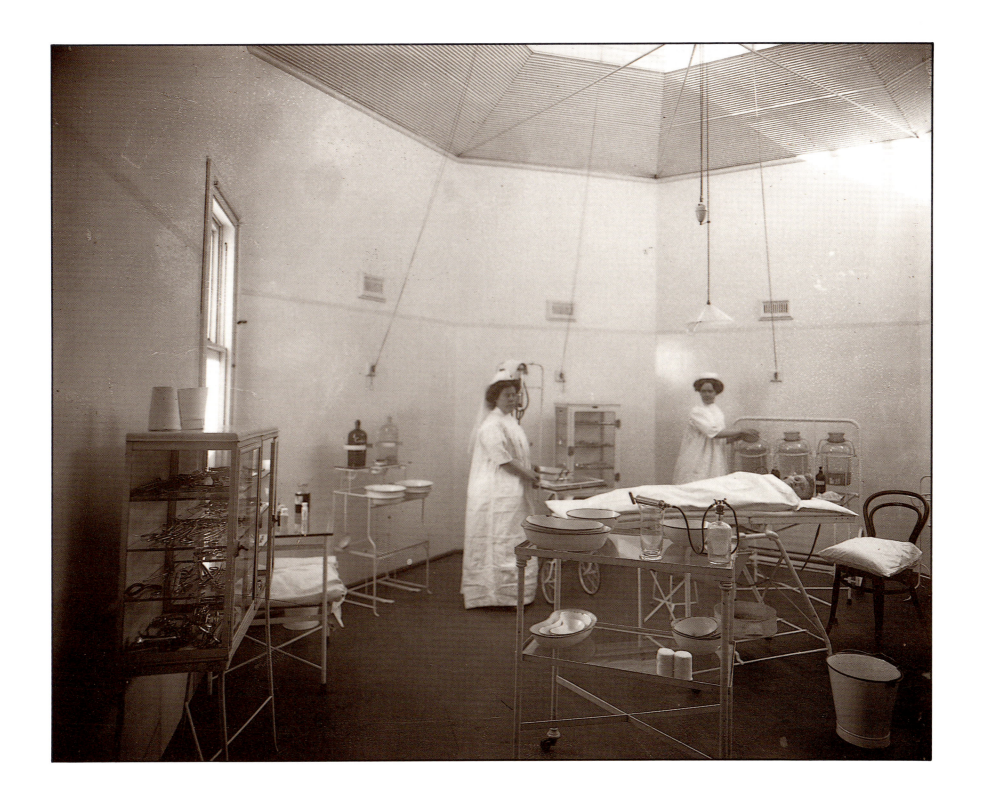

Dr Barber's operating theatre, February 1912

The main ward at the Government Hospital, 1912

63. Bushland around Kalgoorlie after more than a decade of underground mining (GMM 1627)

64. Building a dam with the use of camels 1917 (GMM 1472)

65. The rail track into Lloyd George gold mine 1922 (GMM 1431)

66. Headframe of the Lloyd George mine 1922 (GMM 1331)

67. An elevated railway slices through the Golden Mile 1904 (GMM 2005)

68. Silhouettes amid the mounds at Great Boulder 1905 (GMM 1152)

69. Large buildings and small at the Perseverance gold mine, c1912 (GMM 1483)

70. A lonely patch of water on the Golden Mile, 1905 (GMM 1264)

71. Mammary monuments of soil overshadow a typical Golden Mile operation c1904 (GMM 2011)

72. Industrial landscape at the Golden Mile (GMM 2008)

73. A Golden Mile mine smoking at both ends, 1905, (GMM 2149)

74. Looking South from the Kalgurli gold mine poppet head, 1904 (GMM 1107)

75. A steam train puffs its way past Hannans Star gold mine, 1904, as seen from the yard of Kamballie Station (GMM 1308)

76. The view from the Ivanhoe, with the Great Boulder main shaft headframe in the centre distance c1902 (GMM 1035)

77. Miners drag their feet on the way to work, Great Boulder gold mine, Edwards Shaft, one hazy day in February c1905 (GMM 2010)

78. View from Boulder Main Reef headframe, 1902 (GMM 1036)

79. A trainload of tailings about to be loaded c1904 (GMM 2006)

80. The surface workings of Great Boulder gold mine c1904 (GMM 2012)

81. Tertiary storage bins at the Great Boulder, under construction in 1934 (GMM 1664)

82. The Great Boulder gold mine the morning after a flash flood, viewed from the South East, 1910 (GM 1075)

83. Managers quarters at the Golden Horseshoe gold mine 1909 (GMM 1266)

84. A roller-coaster ride up the tailings dump at the Golden Horseshoe gold mine c1904 (GMM 1339)

85. Golden Horseshoe gold mine engine house (GMM 1251)

86. Conveyor and pump at the Golden Horseshoe gold mine (GMM 1113)

87. The headframe and accompanying mine buildings of the Associated Northern Iron Duke Shaft, 1910 (GMM 1061)

88. February, 1912: Looking East from the Golden Mile out over the Perseverance gold mine and the tiny houses to the expansive bush beyond (GMM 1347)

89. Rebuilding the Oroya, viewed from the South East, 1937: the headframe and the steel bin are new (GMM 1916)

90. A glass house garden in suburban Kalgoorlie (GMM 1518)

91. Potted plants and a cup of tea in the hot sun, North Kalgoorlie School Staff House, 1921 (GMM 1963)

92. A Northwards view of Mt Charlotte and the top of the Golden Mile from above Hannan Street, 1919 (GMM 1045)

93. Goldfields children play on the power cables of Kalgoorlie's Electric Power House the morning after a cyclone, 5 February 1912 (GMM 1452)

The bush around Kalgoorlie was dry, silent, remorseless. (63) Its beauty was unfamiliar to the eastern Australians who joined the rush, although the strange wildflowers were as lavish here as in the country on the other side of Southern Cross, and some of the smaller bushes added yellows and golds to the ochres and greens of the earth and flora. Stands of tall eucalypts enlivened the landscape, and the salt-pans possessed an awesome beauty, but the first Europeans found the region's lack of running water and discernible topography especially daunting. Kalgoorlie was the first Australian settlement built without a recognisable feature of European landscape in view. Other towns were sited on a river or the coast, or at least within sight of a mountain range.

The Golden Mile mining area became a kind of man-made alternative, an artificial range of small hills which signified that the area was now colonised. The cartographers and surveyors quickly laid claim to the area, drawing boundaries on their maps, planting datum pegs in the ground, defining mining leases and deciding where roads would go. But fences and boundaries could never mean much in this kind of landscape, and an overbearing respect for land ownership was never conspicuous on the goldfields.

Water was a problem in this wasteland, If, as Frederic Vosper believed, there had to exist huge reserves of artesian water underneath Kalgoorlie, why build the pipeline all the way from Mundaring Weir? The sheer scale of the water problem made even a simple task like dredging a dam seem a fruitless project. (64)

But the newcomers kept on arriving, and within a decade there were 50,000 people living and working across the goldfields. They were like an army of ants scratching at the surface of an enormous field. Industriously they dug down into the earth and the scree which formed around their holes gave new colours and undulations to the landscape. Roads and tracks were hacked through the bush and headframes appeared everywhere, like matchstick creations, poking out of the scrub at every turn, and even dwarfing the taller eucalypts. (65)

The most dramatic alterations to the environment, however, were on the Golden Mile. Dwyer's photographs of the mines' area are reminiscent of John Beattie's depiction of the western Tasmanian mining towns. This suggests some contact with Beattie when Dwyer was first training as a photographer in Tasmania. (66) As in Beattie's documentation of Queenstown, heaps were identified by Dwyer as dramatic subjects in their own right. He struggled to get a good perspective on these piles of soil, achieving some fine results from the tops of headframes and along elevated railtracks connecting a mine headframe to a treatment plant. (67-68)

In other views, Dwyer emphasised the forest of upright structures which had been planted throughout the Golden Mile: electricity poles, chimney stacks, poppets and all the other perpendiculars of the big mines. (69) In the views of Great Boulder a sense of movement is effectively conveyed. Dwyer was attempting to photograph an intrinsically difficult subject, and there was the danger of rendering this moonscape flat and lifeless, of interest only to the specialist eye. It was also a landscape constantly changing and, in Dwyer's time, made less habitable and rather bleaker by the development of deep-mining. His view of Perseverance from the south-west, taken around 1912, shows that the nearby residential area was becoming well-nigh abandoned.

From inside the very centre of the Golden Mile area, Dwyer produced a series of elegant portraits of the mining landscape. One is almost pastoral in its sympathetic treatment of a pool of water, (70) lines of ridges, telegraph posts (standing in for trees) and the scatter of mine buildings down a distant hillside. There is a careful massing of woodline trucks, power cables, chimneys, buildings and waste dumps in another vignette. (71) A tightly composed view addresses the juxtaposition of stacked timber and chimney stacks. (72) More characteristic of Dwyer's work was the panoramic view from atop a headframe over adjacent workings to the suburban sprawl beyond: in such vistas, the miners' cottages and the shimmering flat horizon are insignificant behind the belching, fuming, depopulated mineworks. (73)

Away to the south of the Golden Mile the housing tapered off quickly. Another view from the top of a poppet, the Kalgurli, showed the interposition of domestic and industrial life on the Golden Mile. A woman hangs out her washing in left-centre; water tubes slither up the condenser plants like mechanical snakes; and in the middle distance a white gaggle of miners' shacks brightens the drab landscape. (74) These shacks were occupied by bachelors, and were later given over to southern European miners, earning for this area the epithet 'Dingbat Flat'.

Not far from here was the Kamballie Railway Station, one of ten in the suburban rail network of Kalgoorlie; the rail system had a greater air of permanence than many other local artefacts. Looking south-west from above the water tank, Dwyer caught an interesting view of the Hannan's Star headframe to the left and headframes used to hoist tailings on the right. (75)

Running in a line from north of Kamballie Station, almost as far up as the Golden Gate Railway Station, the Great Boulder mines were the key operation on the Golden Mile, managed by the rough and capable Richard Hamilton. Naturally Dwyer concentrated a good deal of attention on this area, and in one case, positioned himself atop Ivanhoe to get a clear shot looking east across the main Great Boulder workings. (76) This photograph was taken about 1902. Over to the right, behind the water cooler, is the new headframe of the Golden Horseshoe.

Some years later, in February 1909, he moved in closer to the Edward's shaft to obtain one of his few well-populated mining shots. The arriving shift of miners trudges towards the shaft with that curious eyes-downward gait of the goldfielders. (77)

During the intervening years several new chimneys have sprouted to add further texture to this landscape. Other views of Great Boulder from Chaffers Shaft indicate the steady accumulation of tailing mounds, the thickening forest of chimneys, and the multiplication of railtracks. **(78)** The tailings elevator took the excess material up into mounds, stacked so as to minimise the space required. **(79)** These huge dumps grew under the angle of the elevator, and were not re-treated by the flotation process until the 1930s. Behind the elevator were the tanks and vats, smouldering like witches' cauldrons. **(80-81)** In 1934 slime dumps were built and later photographed by Mackay. A sudden downpour would run straight through the Golden Mile, leaving a streaked pattern in the flats dividing one mining enterprise from the next. **(82)**

The Golden Horseshoe mine was just north of Chaffers Shaft, in the south-western corner of the Golden Mile area. Here trees and the managers' quarters brightened the bleak industrial landscape. Many managers lived on their company's mining lease in order to supervise more closely the activities in their mine. **(83)**

From the other side, the Golden Horseshoe mine looked as bleak as any other, with a roller-coaster of a tailings elevator built over huge dumps. **(84)** Its engine house was a model of goldfields technology and in this and other photographs of machinery, Dwyer emphasized the scale of the technology, dwarfing the humans involved. **(85)** Nineteenth century photographers had sought to picture individual workers against their industrial backdrop, and some of Dwyer's images recall this tradition, but here the machinery itself takes precedence. There seems to be a selfconscious need to assert the advanced state of mining technology in Kalgoorlie. In some views, such as that of the conveyor and pump at the Golden Horseshoe, no humans appear in the picture at all. **(86)**

The Iron Duke headframe of Associated Northern rode high on a sea of tailings. **(87)** The view east over the Perseverance mine caught glimpses of the smaller operations in that part of the Golden Mile, and in the immediate foreground is a condenser. **(88)** It was in this vicinity, at the Oroya, that rebuilding took place in 1937. Mackay's portraits of workers juggling girders and the freshly clad structure evoke the sense of recovery experienced in the gold industry during that decade. **(89)**

In the suburbs on the western edge of the Golden Mile, the landscape could be rendered more attractive to the European eye. After the water supply scheme opened in 1903 enterprising gardeners produced elaborate floral displays. **(90-91)** But from almost every angle of Kalgoorlie was felt the dominating presence of the Golden Mile: hundreds of stamps beat out an incessant and noisy rhythm, the smoke and dust from the mines were a gritty reality and, as a constant reminder of the town's source of weath, Mt Charlotte could be seen from Hannan Street itself. **(92)** Then, just as it seemed man had planted himself firmly in the local environment, a severe storm would lash Kalgoorlie, bringing down the cables and flooding the Golden Mile. **(93)**

Kalgoorlie Bush

Bushland around Kalgoorlie after more than a decade of underground mining 1910

Building a dam with the use of camels 1917

The rail track into Lloyd George gold mine 1922

Headframe of the Lloyd George mine 1922

An elevated railway slices through the Golden Mile 1904

Silhouettes amid the mounds at Great Boulder 1905

Large buildings and small at the Perseverance gold mine, c1912

A lonely patch of water on the Golden Mile, 1905

Mammary monuments of soil overshadow a typical Golden Mile operation c1904

Industrial landscape at the Golden Mile c1904

A Golden Mile mine smoking at both ends 1905

Looking South from the Kalgurli gold mine poppet head, 1904

A steam train puffs its way past Hannans Star gold mine, 1904, as seen from the yard of Kamballie Station

The view from the Ivanhoe, with the Great Boulder main shaft headframe in the centre distance c1902

Miners drag their feet on the way to work, Great Boulder gold mine, Edwards Shaft,
one hazy day in February c1905

Another view of Boulder Main Reef headframe 1902

A trainload of tailings about to be loaded c1904

The surface workings of Great Boulder gold mine c1904

Tertiary storage bins at the Great Boulder, under construction in 1934

The Great Boulder gold mine the morning after a flash flood, viewed from the South East, 1910

Managers quarters at the Golden Horseshoe gold mine c1907

A roller-coaster ride up the tailings dump at the Golden Horseshoe gold mine c1904

Golden Horseshoe gold mine engine house c1909

Conveyor and pump at the Golden Horseshoe gold mine c1909

The headframe and accompanying mine buildings of the Associated Northern Iron Duke Shaft, 1910

February, 1912: Looking East from the Golden Mile out over the Perseverance gold mine
and the tiny houses to the expansive bush beyond

Rebuilding the Oroya, viewed from the South East, 1937: the headframe and the steel bin are new

A glass house garden in suburban Kalgoorlie

Potted plants and a cup of tea in the hot sun

A Northwards view of Mt Charlotte and the top of the Golden Mile from above Hannan Street

Goldfields children play on the power cables of Kalgoorlie's Electric Power House
the morning after a cyclone, 5 February 1912

Hannan Street began life as an informal venue for conversation and other necessities, any pretensions to a thoroughfare interrupted both by trees which had to be navigated, and by its sudden end at Mt Charlotte. (94) The trees of Hannan Street were replaced by electric wires which formed a line of sentinels down the middle of the road; and by the time Dwyer's name had been replaced by that of Mackay high above the street, its classic appearance had been established. (95) It had become the commercial and administrative focus of the entire goldfields, the visible evidence of the region's prosperity.

Yet it was still a meeting place, where locals could get together in hotels or hairdressing salons, a place of conversation under the shelter of the verandahs and companionship on the balconies which girded each pub. Hannan Street became a classic main thoroughfare of the Australian Outback.

The street had many moods which Dwyer, living above his premises near the intersection with Maritana Street, knew well. On race-days it was abuzz with crowded trams, well-dressed young men in boaters or bowlers, and lost children. (96) On weekdays, in the late morning, it was businesslike, with drays ferrying goods in and out of stores, or crowded with men talking, laying plans or discussing current affairs. (97) Street conversation was an important means of communication before the widespread use of the telephone, and it was not regarded as odd for men to sit down in the street, a habit that lent a relaxed atmosphere to public places. (98)

When the football or the races were finished, and late afternoon shadows lengthened on the pavement, the buzz was gone, replaced by the mellow sound of a happily-tired crowd reviewing the favourites who didn't win or the certain goals mis-kicked. By 1905 the hills around Kalgoorlie had been shaved clean of the bristle of trees seen in the photograph of 1895. (99)

At the intersection of Hannan and Maritana Streets, Dwyer took an unusual picture of a speeding car, the vehicle a mere blur as it negotiated the bend. Cyclists and pedestrians alike have stopped to stare, while some onlookers are standing in the middle of the road, a practice soon to become impractical, though few would have realised that at the time. Several pedestrians are gripping the brims of their hats, either as a mark of respect to the car or for fear that the sudden gust of wind would render them hatless. The driver and passengers have lost their identity and they too are a blur. (100)

Cars represented one symbol of urban life in Kalgoorlie; another was the increase in more permanent housing, as the suburbs grew on the northern slopes and south towards Boulder. The price of a house was relatively cheap when set against a miner's wages, and a 1907 photograph of a Hannan Street estate agent gives details of prices ranging from 100 to 475 pounds. (101) At this time the lowest-paid miner earned 11/8 per eight-hour shift, and the average weekly pay for miners was 3/12/-, but the chance of obtaining a loan to purchase a house was very poor.

When mine jobs were available, a man could maintain a respectable standard of living although the cost of perishable goods was high. Clothes on sale in Hannan Street suggested that some of Kalgoorlie's residents were able to afford good quality fashion. (102) Every family had its 'Sunday best', and it was often only in these clothes that people were photographed. (103)

To shop in Hannan Street was to see a range and quality of goods equal to that found in any major Australian city of the day. Chairs and dresses of all shapes and sizes were available, and while most day-to-day clothes were handmade by women at home, shops selling cheap factory-made clothes gradually replaced them. Male assistants had the task of measuring and cutting of fabric, (104) and were expected to stand while the customer sat. Handling money was not their duty as it was sent aloft via the change-machine to clerks elsewhere in the store.

Big retailers such as Bairds, did well in Kalgoorlie. Ballarat-born William Hutchison Baird was remembered as 'a natural merchandiser' whose skills in hardware were extended into general retailing. His Perth store promised everything 'from needles to windmills' and the Bairds later became a Peppermint Grove clan.

Modern banking facilities were available, including a local branch of the Commonwealth Bank, a Labor-inspired government bank which sought to set a standard for the dozen or so private banks in a city the size of Kalgoorlie. Both men and women were employed by banks, but tellers were men. It was a good career for the academically-minded, and even for the young man who had both hearing and sight impairments. (105) Kalgoorlie bank Johnnies of the 1890s wore handguns but a mesh screen was considered adequate protection.

Hannan Street also boasted the City Markets, established in 1901 between Cassidy and Wilson Streets — a good source of fresh food, including recently-slain poultry at Christmas time. These were the days when fresh food and newsprint still went together. (106)

The presentation of goods for sale followed several clear conventions. Women's clothes were displayed with more imagination than men's, as women were more difficult to persuade. **(107)** Men's clothes and grocery items were placed in neat rows covering the walls — as in the careful alignment of cans and bottles at Fernies Store, drawing on the metaphor of the well-stocked pantry. **(108)**

These stores gradually became more attractive and less functional with the development of poster advertising, tiled floors, and even potted plants. Southern Europeans, especially Greeks like the Kalaf family, began taking over this line of business in the 1920s, and there was hardly an Australian country town in the inter-war period which could not boast a Greek-owned cafe.

In 1934 the Greek owner of a Kalgoorlie wine saloon issued a notice disavowing any connection with the growing 'foreigner' community, but to no avail, as his business was pillaged along with all the others in the Australia Day riots of that year.

Later in 1934 the Kalaf family attempted a more subtle approach to proving their bona fides with the Anglo-Australian customers — the donation of a football premiership trophy. **(109)**

Over at the men's clothiers of John R. Saunders, business continued as usual. This was a working-man's style of store (though Saunders lived in Mullingar), and the clothes were laid out to fill the whole window. **(110)** Saunders, a Labor supporter, emigrated to Perth, where a chain of his down-to-earth stores became dotted through the working-class suburbs.

The street life of men never took them far from the hotel, a pivotal institution in Kalgoorlie's social history. **(111)** By 1903 there were 92 pubs in the town, serving a total population of about 28,000 people, 7,000 of whom were miners. There were roughly 100 'regulars' for each pub, making hotels a lucrative business indeed. Many astute leaders, including politicians, had a financial interest in a pub; it was widely believed that Philip Collier had a half-share in a Wiluna hotel, and such involvement was certainly not regarded as a repudiation of a man's Labor credentials. The situation made the struggle of barmen and barmaids difficult (barmaids achieved equal pay in Western Australia in 1911).

A large army of serving staff was needed to sell, package and deliver consumer goods in old Kalgoorlie, providing a useful source of employment. Frank William Bricknell, JP, who lived in Mullingar, ran a busy Hannan Street firm catering for banquets such as those which celebrated Lord Hopetoun's 1902 visit and the opening of the water scheme. **(112)** The latter *'lasted five hours, fifty cases of champagne were consumed, and a ton of ice was needed to keep the proceedings from becoming over-heated'*! Bricknell sold his store fittings in 1918-19 and became a baker in Aberdeen Street, Perth.

Before the development of gassed beer, a bottle would lose its 'fizz' after 24 hours, and this technical limitation necessitated a brewery in every locality. Kalgoorlie itself had eight in 1903, and even towns as close as Kanowna boasted their own. Each brewery gave employment to many men, some of whom undertook the repetitive work of sealing bottles, a process that was not fully automated until the 1920s. **(113)**

Transporting commodities was a slow, laborious and expensive process, the crucial factor being the distance from rail. The transcontinental railway, though promised about the time Dwyer arrived in Kalgoorlie, was not completed until the year he departed. Even mail from Hannan Street, which only travelled a block or two by horse and dray before being loaded on to the train, was not guaranteed a speedy journey. **(114)** Local wags said the WAGR emblazoned on each carriage must have stood for 'Walk and Go Rapidly'. The goldfields' mail system had taken so long to set up that entrepreneurs in the 1890s established bicycle versions of the Pony Express. **(115)** Although these methods of transport did not last long into the twentieth century, the bike was still regarded as a symbol of efficiency and speed; and even the humble horse, plodding along Kalgoorlie's streets with a dray of cumbersome or heavy items was indispensable until replaced by the truck. Richard (Dick) Pascoe was one such carrier, running delivery errands such as a drayload of mining tools from Harris Scarfe to the Golden Mile. Pascoe walked his horse and kept a lively dog for company on the road. **(116)**

Everyday transport needs were met by the Loop trains and the trams. Like other major cities, including Fremantle and Perth, Kalgoorlie had an extensive network, established in 1902, with eighteen electric trams bumping along about fifteen miles of suburban track. When the staff were taken to dinner by the management, it was held in the tram-barn, with a 'Boulder City' tram to keep them company. **(117)**

Dwyer's images of the local business houses reflect the older relationship between an employer and his workers. Examples of these classic photographs survive from almost every nineteenth-century industrial city around Australia. The boss sits, or is positioned, in the middle of the fellows, who stand in a long line stretching the length of the premises.

Often, as at the Bottling works a child or a pet is included in the picture. **(118)** This apparently spontaneous gesture conveys the sense of a 'family' business. At the Langford Brewery the formula is repeated, but without the children, and with one worker (left) looking decidedly left out of the otherwise jolly proceedings. **(119)** The boss is surrounded by the rest of the manual workers, while the office employees keep their distance from the blue-collar types. Dwyer's copy of an 1894 view of the Post Office indicates that the public (again including children) could be ranged in like fashion outside a local institution. **(120)**

The sense of 'home' was difficult for a goldfields' photographer to capture, as there were few permanent houses. Because so many goldfields' residents regularly changed their address with a new job, or a new mine, houses were designed and built so that they could simply be hauled to the new site. **(121)**

Sometimes houses were dismembered, each part carefully numbered, and re-assembled in Perth or Fremantle. There could be confusions in this process: when the Pells left Mullingar their house did not show up in suburban Darlington and it took many solicitous enquiries before it was discovered — in Esperance!

The interior of Kalgoorlie's 'best' homes were not as lavish or as well-appointed as those in the affluent suburbs of Perth, but were equally tasteful by contemporary standards, adorned with Aboriginal artefacts and framed photographs.

Aboriginal *objects d'art* took pride of place in the entrance hall, a significant mark of respect; and those two essential elements of late-Victorian decor, the crowded mantelpiece and the piano, were both in evidence. **(122)** Mrs Alicia Pell remembered the social significance of the piano in her reminiscences:

> *My mother had insisted on bringing over our piano from Victoria and it was one of the few owned privately in 1897. It was a great magnet and many jolly sing-songs we had in the evenings.*[2]

Luxurious conditions also prevailed in hotel and railway diningrooms. **(123)**

Horses were still a part of everyday life, particularly in mine work. They were kept underground and used to haul trolleys, being brought up to the surface only for medical attention or during the summer holidays; during these times they were blind-folded and very gradually exposed to sunlight. **(124)** Motor cars became more widely accepted during the First World War, and were bought by a growing number of Kalgoorlie residents.**(125-126)**

Other signs of technological change became evident in everyday life, but traditional enterprises, such as Dunne's Bakery, were still using nineteenth-century technology. **(127)** The dental surgery used electricity for light and heat and had a water supply, but the drills were pedal-driven. **(128)**

Commercial buildings in central Kalgoorlie became grander and laneways were lined with stone pitches. **(129)** These buildings were seen as durable in a way that factories were not, and even a large manufacturing establishment, such as Hannan's Brewery (in which Dwyer had shares), was brick only in its central portion. **(130)** Its remaining buildings were galvanised iron stretched over a wood or steel framework. By contrast, the flour mills erected at the same time in the wheat belt of Western Australia, were generally brick, evidence of the common assumption of the day — that gold was only a temporary industry. The horse and dray were used for deliveries from the brewery to the hotels, outside which the horse and dray looked rather incongruous alongside the cars. **(131)**

The first service stations were positioned on the main streets, under the verandahs of major hotels, such as the Maritana Street side of the Palace, occupying a position far more prominent than the livery stables had ever done. The James and Pollock Garage was located in Hannan Street itself. **(132)**

Kalgoorlie became a major way-station on the rigorous 'transcontinental' journey described by the Royal Automobile Club booklets issued annually from about 1915. Driving conditions were arduous, but seemed comfortable by the standards of camel travel. Motorists cleaned their vehicles specially for the camera, and promotional material suggested that even this irksome business could be automated, an idea which would appeal to residents of a dusty town like Kalgoorlie. **(133)** For the same reason interior photographs showed rugs over linoleum, a sensible arrangement in those adverse conditions.

Everyday life in old Kalgoorlie changed rapidy from the time Dwyer arrived, and by the time he left it was no longer an Outback settlement. Living conditions had improved greatly, but at the cost of certain unique values: 'The Boulder had gone down', as one old-time poet put it. Changes in technology were the external indications of more basic alterations in social life. The easy-going frontier days were rapidly being replaced by a community which had 'settled down'.

---

[2] 'Reminiscences of Alice Pell' (Mss, Battye Library, Perth).

The beginnings of ''Hannans Street, Kalgurli'', c1895

One of Mackay's first portraits of the street, 1917, his own name having superseded
that of Dwyer in the sign above the building

A raceday crush at the main corner, Hannan and Maritana Streets

Looking west from just above Maritana Street

Outside the Palace Hotel

The view of Hannan Street east from Cassidy Street

Pedestrians and cyclists are unmoving while a blurred car rounds the corner of
Maritana and Hannan Streets

Real estate notices outside the Goldfields Building Society, May 1907

The shop window of Brennan Brothers

Noland's second-hand sales and auction room

Attentive sales assistants at Brennan Brothers

Offices of the newly-formed Commonwealth Bank c1911

Poultry shop at the Kalgoorlie City Markets, Hannan Street

Interior of women's fashion store

Neat rows of grocery items, Fernies Store

The Kalaf family desire to be accepted, 1934

A potpourri of men's personal items at the long-running store of John R. Saunders

Pausing for a drink outside the Great Boulder Hotel

Established in 1897, Frank W. Bricknell's Hannan Street business was booming

Sealing the bottles, Standard Brewery, Kanowna, in October 1907

About to despatch the mail bags from the Kalgoorlie Post Office, Hannan Street

Two cyclists who ride the Davies Franklin brand, August 1909

Dick Pascoe and his dog outside the mining equipment supplier, George P. Harris Scarfe

A staff dinner for the Kalgoorlie Tramway Company, 13 September 1907

The boss of the Bottling Works and his employees, 1909

Langfords Brewery staff

The original Hannans Post and Telegraph Office, 1894

Transporting the house of Dr Walker in May 1911

The lounge room of Mr W. Leslie at 37 Lewis Street, Kalgoorlie, April 1908

The interior of a railway dining car 1912

A veterinarian examines a horse in his crush, April 1907

An elderly Kalgoorlie beau arrives in his Studebaker, 1916

The Goodal family and their Hubmobile

Pastrycooks at Dunne's bakery, May 1912

Visiting the dentist, July 1907

The AMP building

Wagons loaded with beer barrels outside Hannans Brewery

A 1925 Paige and a 1923 Jowett parked outside Greenwood's Grand Hotel in Hannan Street

The James and Pollock Garage in Hannan Street

Mr Shaw and his car

5 GROWING UP IN OLD KALGOORLIE

134. Studio portrait of Baby Truman, 17 August 1909 (GMM 2944)

135. A studio portrait of Master Egan, 10 December 1907 (GMM 1574)

136. Dwyer's collage of "The Rising Generation — Youthful Goldfields Residents", 1903 (GMM 1315)

137. Anglican Sunday School group (GMM 2051)

138. Young thespians dressed for a harvest performance (GMM 2056)

139. Children dress up in goldfields family portrait 1921 (GMM 1309)

140. Mr A. Griffiths and the Kalgoorlie Junior Football Club, posed for premiership memento in September 1914. (GMM 1230)

141. Cyclists prepare for road race from outside Criterion Hotel 1909 (GMM 1090)

142. Roman Catholic convent group (GMM 2146)

143. Class at St Anthony's Convent school, Coolgardie, 1907 (GMM 1633)

144. Christian Brothers College Gymnastics Team, 1910 (GMM 1554)

145. The new Australian flag on a may-pole at North Kalgoorlie Primary School, 1921 (GMM 1451)

146. A child's birthday party 1922 (GMM 1955)

147. Children lead the St Patrick's Day procession, Burt Street (GMM 2121)

148. Two young girls posed behind the Golden Eagle nugget, January 1931 (GMM 1129)

Children were an unplanned part of old Kalgoorlie. The goldfields were the province of bachelors who gave little thought to such matters. The open availability of prostitutes meant that sex and procreation could be regarded as separate activities; and this was as true for women as for men, because it was partly the prostitutes who first learnt about the new contraceptive methods which gained currency at the end of the nineteenth century.

Children rarely figure in the 'manly' bush balladry for which Kalgoorlie is well known. This is not to say that children were unwanted or unloved; their studio portraits are as sentimental as anywhere else in Australia at the time. (134, 135) Rather, as elsewhere, it was assumed that children

would not deflect parents far from their own ambitions; instead, the needs of offspring were subordinated to those of parents. More importantly, Edwardian-age parents believed that they could direct their children's careers and values fairly closely. Childhood possessed less autonomy than it would have at the end of the twentieth century, and Kalgoorlie parents had not moved far beyond the older idea that children were simply adults-in-process. (136) One of the clearest signs of this was the enthusiasm with which the new child cadet scheme (1911) and the Boy Scouts were received in Kalgoorlie. These were British-Imperial developments which moved to their logical conclusion with 'the War'.

Goldfields' parents in fact received less assistance in child-rearing from their own parents than was customary. With no grandparents in Kalgoorlie, the first diggers and their wives raised their children without the pool of traditional folklore which is normally part of each generation's heritage. Church groups had some influence on children's values, but it was minimal among the Protestants. (137) One boy whose parents had come from Britain in 1911 explained their attitude in these terms:

Although professing Anglicans, neither father nor mother were what were commonly known as 'church-goers'. Nevertheless, mother sent my sister and me to Sunday School whenever she could. She never seemed to mind what denomination Sunday School we attended or where she went herself on the rare occasions that she took it into her head to go to church. Anywhere would do so long as it was not Catholic. Like many another she was a WASP (white Anglo-Saxon Protestant) from conditioning rather than conviction.

Because of his British background, Norman Bartlett's memories are sometimes different from those of Gavin Casey, although they grew up in at the same time, Casey was born Kalgoorlie itself in 1907, and his outlook was more typical — a fusion of the local and the British.

Remembers Bartlett:

One could even play Indians alone, sitting stripped to the waist, daubed with crayon, real feathers in braided hair, smoking a pipe of peace made from a cork or a conker with hoarded cool-drink straw, refusing to communicate with parents, sister or visitors with more than the traditional 'Ugh! Ugh!' [1]

Kalgoorlie lacked many of the facilities for children available in capital cities — there was only one library, no swimming pool for many years, and no museum — and they were, to a large extent, thrown back on their own resources. Theatre was one significant aspect of their lives, **(138)** and they took pleasure in dressing up. **(139)**

When the cinema arrived, it was instantly popular with Bartlett's and Casey's generation, reinforcing some of the British and American material they were reading:

Most small boys passed through the Saturday afternoon picture phase. For threepence at the Majestic Theatre in Hannan Street we could see Tom Mix, Hoot Gibson, or William S. Hart in the first Westerns. A lady pianist followed the action with the Light Cavalry music or the William Tell Overture, accompanied perhaps by a powerful chorus of 'Shut the door!' as some child wandered out into the side alley and let in the light. [2]

Another popular activity was sport; both boys and girls of the goldfields took an active interest in tennis, cricket and Australian Rules football. **(140)** The passion for Australian Rules was natural, given the preponderance of Victorians on the goldfields. It was also a simple game that could be played by many or few, without much equipment. Kalgoorlie produced many champions of the game. Cycling was extremely popular, rivalling pastimes which later superseded it. At the start of a great cycling race outside the Criterion Hotel in about 1922, the boys lined up for a group portrait. Some fidgetted, and their bikes wobbled while onlookers clustered around them, helping to maintain their position. Two of the riders wore knotted handkerchiefs to protect themselves against the sun. **(141)**

But the great pleasure for Kalgoorlie boys of Gavin Casey's generation and disposition, was the Dumps area:

Roaming the Dumps would be other small boys in the rig of the day, cheap cotton 'jumpers' and short denim pants, and when your mob met up with them, after an exchange of pleasantries, positions of advantage would be taken up and a slime fight would follow. The lumps of dried slime, broken to size in the hand, made an admirable form of ammunition. They broke on impact, with harm to no one except to all

when they got home. The chip bath-heater would be stoked up and an angry mother would make you wash your clothes as well as yourself. On the Dumps, too, were switchback bike-pads winding between abandoned shafts and mullock-tips; and if you were lucky and owned a 'grid' you flew around the blind turns with the wind in your ears and your heart in your mouth, dreaming of Major Segrave and Kaye Don at Brooklands. [3]

At school, the children received a strict and inflexible education, both in government and Catholic schools. After 1911 all boys had to attend a national cadet scheme, a course of paramilitary training which prepared them practically and psychologically for the supposedly inevitable global conflict. Young Catholic children also underwent an important socialization in the sodalities. These were religious societies, established by schools and orphanages, which provided rules and habits designed to help young people to become good Catholics. A popular sodality at this time, the Children of Mary, set down in a manual rules and advice on how a girl might express her devotion to the Virgin Mary in her daily life. **(142)**

A convent school education was rigorous, producing young women capable of deep commitment. The best-regarded example on the goldfields was St Anthony's at Coolgardie, to which many Catholic families for miles around sent their children. Many schoolchildren were musical, like Kalgoorlie pianist Eileen Joyce; others became educators themselves or entered the religious life.

Classrooms were festooned with the powerful icons of Roman Catholicism, and students sat in straight lines. **(143)** The Christian Brothers College at Kalgoorlie offered a more physical, less devotional and meditative education, priding itself on its gymnastics team. **(144)** Government schools had similar classrooms but here the icons were secular, like copies of the Dutch Old Masters. The deity was the new nationalism of the period, expressed in events such as the dance around a pole draped in the new Australian flag. This North Kalgoorlie primary school dance had first been practised indoors. **(145)**

Outside school, there were three great influences on the children of old Kalgoorlie. One was their training as boys and girls, in which they were given fairly definite gender roles, even in the simple pleasures of childhood such as the birthday party. **(146)**

---

[1] Norman Bartlett, *Quadrant* (June 1978) pp. 35-36.

[2] Gavin Casey and Ted Mayman, *The Mile That Midas Touched* (Rigby, Adelaide, 1964) p. 168.

[3] ibid., pp. 169-170.

It was harder for girls growing up on the goldfields than it was for boys. Flaming Youth and the Roaring Twenties were not for Kalgoorlie, where poverty and a heavy pall of Victorianism hung over many middle-class homes. There were a few jobs as shop assistants for some of the daughters, but the demand for school teachers and nurses and other professions was limited. To be a music-teacher or a missionary seemed a popular ambition for elder sisters. Most girls were well trained in domestic duties by their mothers, took lessons in arts and crafts, music, and drawing, and stayed to help in the home, with matrimony somewhere in a vague future . . .[4]

The second influence was the ethnic imperative of belonging to either the Protestant tribe or the Catholic one. The St Patrick's Day procession down Burt Street began with children at the head. **(147)** Every procession attracted Kalgoorlie lads wanting to get in on the act, riding their billy-goat carts at the very rear of the march:

The goats often obstinately refused to enter into the spirit of the thing, and jibbed and bucked and pranced about, but the young owners had just as good a time as anyone else.[5]

But the third influence was the most important: goldfields children grew up knowing the value of the search for that precious metal which had brought their parents to this desolate part of Australia. **(148)** It was a search which gave their lives some purpose and themselves some identity as goldfielders.

Perhaps the yarns, half overheard and only half understood by kids listening to their dads talk with friends, were unconsciously embroidered in the telling, for men in mining towns are honest liars when they talk about gold, but at least the local history and the stories enriched the atmosphere for children after the first World War in that otherwise drab and dusty town.[6]

---

[4] ibid., p. 173

[5] ibid., p. 172

[6] ibid., pp. 167-168

Studio portrait of Baby Truman, 17 August 1909

A studio portrait of Master Egan, 10 December 1907

Dwyer's collage of "The Rising Generation — Youthful Goldfields Residents", 1903

Anglican Sunday School group

Young thespians dressed for a harvest performance

Children dress up in goldfields family portrait 1921

Mr A. Griffiths and the Kalgoorlie Junior Football Club, posed for
premiership memento in September 1914

Cyclists prepare for tour from outside Criterion Hotel c1909

Roman Catholic sodality group

Class at St Anthony's Convent school, Coolgardie, 1907

Christian Brothers College Gymnastics Team, 1910

The new Australian flag on a may-pole at North Kalgoorlie Primary School

A child's birthday party

Children lead the St Patrick's Day procession, Burt Street

Two young girls posed behind the Golden Eagle nugget Jan. 1931

6 POLITICS AND CULTURE

149. A worker takes time off from the construction of a new headframe and treatment at the Iron Duke to read, 1904 (GMM 1619)

150. St. Patrick's Day Procession, Burt St, Boulder (GMM 2117)

151. The headquarters of the Amalgamated Miners' Association (GMM 2116)

152. A mass meeting of striking woodcutters, 2 August 1908, addressed by Julian Stuart, MLA for Leonora (GMM 1443)

153. A crowd gathers at Hannan Street to read the results of the Federal election, 1913 (GMM 1427)

154. The Executive Council of the Goldfields Reform League, 1900 (Copy of original photo) (GMM 1363)

155. Laying the foundation stone for the Boulder City Town Hall in December 1907 (GMM 1297)

156. Ada Crossley breaks convention by going underground at the Golden Horseshoe gold mine 1904 (GMM 1063)

157. The Boulder Carnival fair-ground stall of the Rechabites, located behind the Boulder Town Hall (GMM 2097)

158. An office of the Mechanics Institute, 1909, called a Miners Institute when it opened in 1895, and used by the local council until 1897 (GMM 1467)

159. The billiards room, 1909 (1904-1957) was located in the galvanized iron hall erected at the back of the Institute in time for the banquet to celebrate the coming of the train in 1896 (GMM 1131)

160. Miners browse through magazines and newspapers in the Reading Room 1909 (GMM 1281)

161. Reading on the first-floor verandah of the Institute overlooking Hannan Street 1917 (GMM 1459)

162. Maurice Geraldo and "The Juggling Geraldos" and others advertised on the billboard of the Cremorne Gardens, 1907 (GMM 1566)

163. A performance at the opening of new Boulder Town Hall on 23 June 1908 (GMM 1476)

164. "Hollister Fashion Plates" — Dwyer Index Fancy Dress Group, 1922 (Copy by MacKay) (GMM 1226)

165. A day at Kalgoorlie Race Course in 1914 (GMM 1299)

166. Flappers and other fashionable types at the Boulder Cup meeting at Boulder Race Course in 1925 (GMM 2094)

167. Leaving a football match, 22 September 1907, Hainault v Boulder (GMM 1437)

168. Afternoon shadows fall across a goldfields bowling green 1912 (GMM 1096)

169. A soldier and the memory of his father, copy for "Way", dated 1920, original photographer unknown (GMM 1477)

The first diggers were usually literate, and some were very well educated people, having grown up in the Australian colonies since the introduction of compulsory schooling in the 1870s. The goldfields were rich in newspapers: in 1903 Kalgoorlie alone had five papers, an extraordinary output for such an isolated industrial town. The *Kalgoorlie Miner* and the *Westralian Worker* were the most durable, but there were numerous others, and Kalgoorlie men played a significant role in the development of a Western Australian press generally. One such man was Billy Clare (1863-1940), founder and owner of the *Coolgardie Miner*; another was R. C. Spear, who from 1906 to 1946 edited the annual journal *Golden West* which carried a great deal of goldfields' material. The *Westralian Worker*, whose most famous editor was John Curtin, later moved to Perth. Vosper started the *Sunday Times* in Perth in 1897 after a period as a journalist on the goldfields. (Of course, only an athiest like Vosper would have dreamt of producing a paper on the Sabbath!)

These newspapers accurately mirrored Kalgoorlie society in the pre-war period: aggressively masculine, cheerfully laconic, determinedly irreverent. They were gossipy about local news, but their reporting of new strikes was compulsory reading for the goldseekers.

The poetry published in these papers represents some of the best Australian creative writing of any place or period. Clare, Emmerson and others were conscious of the part newspapers like the *Bulletin* played in promoting Australian literature and consciously emulated the practice in Western Australia. Poets and journalists of the goldfields were never far removed from the gritty realities of life working on the Golden Mile or prospecting on the baking plains around Kalgoorlie. Newspapers were read at the mines during 'smoko', and offered a moment of quiet in a busy and noisy day. **(149)**

The Kalgoorlie goldfields also provided material for many contemporary novelists. These included Nat Gould, *The Miner's Cup: A Coolgardie Romance* (1896); Hume Nisbet, *The Swampers: A Romance of the Westralian Goldfields* (1897); John Arthur Barry, *The Luck of the Native Born* (1898/99); and Hubert Stewart, *Ungodly Man* (1904). The rush also provided material for the theatre, with dramatic renditions in Euston Leigh and Cyril Clare's London production of *The Duchess of Coolgardie*; (1896) and Louis Esson's account of prospecting in 'The Battler' (1921). In 1907 the popular novelist Arthur Wright wrote *Keane of Kalgoorlie*, which became a film in 1911. Later Richard Donald Lane wrote *The Romance of Old Coolgardie* (1929), a factual novel. Two decades after leaving the photographic business he had inherited from Dwyer, Stuart Gore wrote a popular novel *Down the Golden Mile* (1962), set partly in the goldfields.

Among the best goldfields' poets was Edwin Greenslade Murphy (1861-1939), better known as 'Dryblower'. A Victorian who went prospecting on the fields in 1893, Murphy's poetry was lively and topical, dealing with everyday concerns of the workers. For 40 years he wrote a column 'Verse and Worse' in the *Sunday Times*, from which two anthologies were compiled: *Jarrahland Jingles* (1908), and *Dryblower's Verses 1894-1926* (1926).

Other poets often used pseudonyms, such as 'The Exile', 'The Prodigal' (Dorham Doolette), 'Temora', 'Mulga Mick' (M. J. O'Reilly), and 'Crosscut' (T. H. Wilson). Julian Stuart (1866-1929) called himself 'Curlew' when writing in the eastern colonies, while out west he became 'Saladin'. He edited the *Westralian Worker* from 1903 to 1906, became an MLA, and was later a government clerk. His best-known poem pithily sums up much of the thinking of this 'manly' school of poets:

> I am deformed by labor
> I am the working man
> Cursing the fate that holds me
> A dull-browed Caliban.

The finest creative expression of goldfields' life, however, came later, in Katherine Susannah Prichard's famous trilogy, *The Roaring Nineties* (1946), *Golden Miles* (1948) and *Winged Seeds* (1950) and in Casey's famous *Short Shift Saturday* collection. The various works of non-fiction concerning the goldfields include Malcolm Uren's *Glint of Gold* (1948), Clive Turnbull's biography *Frontier: The Story of Paddy Hannan* (1949), *The Mile that Midas Touched* (1964) by Gavin Casey and Ted Mayman, and the various books and articles by Norma King, H. H. Wilson, Beverley Smith, and others.[1]

Literary culture was tied to a strong sense of political involvement. This was manifest in organized rituals such as the Eight Hour Day processions and the St Patrick's Day march. **(150)** The former, the local equivalent of Europe's May Day, remembered the winning of the Eight Hour Day in Victoria in 1856. St Patrick's Day, March 17, was partly a celebration of Irishness, and partly an affirmation of local collectivity. Unions were primarily an expression of pride in one's work, of confidence in the skills which that work represented and of the product manufactured. Floats displayed specific examples of the item produced by each union.

There were two major miners' unions during the early years. The Amalgamated Miners' Association had a building more permanent and more imposing then any of the neighbouring structures, signifying the place of the union in men's lives. **(151)**

When a strike occurred on the goldfields the consequences were severe as goldfielders were natural unionists and strong militants. In July, 1908, for example, the woodcutters struck over wages and conditions. This was a major industrial dispute involving three companies: the Kalgoorlie-Boulder Firewood Supply Company, the Westralia Firewood and Timber Supply Company and the WA Goldfields Firewood Supply Company. The Lakeside, Kurrawang and Kuramia lines were all affected.

The men had no union representation and rejected the rulings of Arbitration, and the underground mine workings and the ore-reduction processes both came to a standstill. All credit from Perth and Fremantle retailers to goldfields merchants ceased and, to add to the general sense of panic, the electricity supply was in jeopardy. The Labor members of the Legislative Assembly — particularly Bath, Collier, Walker and Stuart — offered themselves as representatives of the woodcutters, and Stuart addressed the men on 2 August. **(152)** Norbert Keenan, once Mayor of Kalgoorlie, and by now the State's Attorney General, made an unsuccessful attempt to resolve the dispute. Finally the Premier, Newton Moore, intervened, offering major concessions to the woodcutters. After 1908 they had union representation and their next major dispute was not until 1919.

---

1 William H. Wilde, Joy Hooton and Barry Andrews, *The Oxford Companion to Australian Literature* (Oxford University Press, Melbourne, 1985) pp. 298-300.

These and other disputes at Kalgoorlie indicated the strength of concerted crowd action on the goldfields, and the reluctance of politicians to offend the goldfielders. This did not save the region, however, when successive State Governments failed to subsidise the industry.

Much of Kalgoorlie's politics was outdoor, such as the conscription referenda, both clear 'No!' votes; despite the efforts of the militarists, goldfields' people could not accept that compulsion was required to get young men to serve in the war. The crowd awaiting the posting of the results filled Hannan Street: it was an anxious moment, with one man (left foreground) nervously twirling his cane, and others surging forward. **(153)**

The goldfields had experienced men on its Reform League at the turn of the century, and a succession of local businessmen in municipal government. **(154)** Boulder, more working-class than Kalgoorlie, laid the foundation stone of its Town Hall in December 1907. **(155)**

The women of Kalgoorlie were not very successful in achieving formal recognition, as the day of an elected woman was still decades away, but some achieved prominence. Visiting female performers included Melba, various actresses, and the contralto Ada Crossley, who sang at Her Majesty's Theatre on the night of 10 January, 1904. During her visit Ada ventured down into the Golden Horseshoe mine with its manager, J. W. Sutherland (seated right), **(156)** something of an honour as women were not often allowed down into a mine.

Most active women of the day concerned themselves with moral persuasion, such as the WCTU or the Rechabites, setting up stalls at events such as the Boulder Carnival. **(157)**

A central cultural institution in everyday life was the Mechanics Institute in Hannan Street. **(158)** Furnished with enormous oval and rectangular billiard tables, its function was partly recreational; **(159)** but it was essentially the intellectual centre of the town, a place where studious young types like Gavin Casey whiled away their spare time reading their way through the novels carefully arranged in alphabetical order. The newspapers for which Kalgoorlie was famous could be perused in the Institute's Reading Room, **(160)** while out on the verandah overlooking Hannan Street, comfortable chairs were available for the same purpose. **(161)** This was a reading culture, a society in which men and women endured hot idle days with the aid of plenty of literature. A quiet smoke or a game of billiards could be enjoyed as well.

Entertainment came in many forms. Vaudeville and jugglers performed at the Cremorne Gardens, **(162)** while dramatic productions brought hundreds into the Boulder Town Hall. **(163)** Amateur groups dollied themselves up in an age when popular theatre was an unselfconscious affair. **(164)** Race-days were popular in every goldfields' town, particularly such highlights as the Boulder Cup. **(165-166)** On these occasions women and men showed off their best and most fashionable clothes, and the 1920's 'flappers' looked nothing like their dowdy mothers of the pre-war period.

Since the quest for gold was largely a matter of luck, it was not surprising that gambling in all its forms was a constant feature of Kalgoorlie life. Two-up, the quintessential Australian gambling game, was such a permanent presence in the goldfields that the State Government finally legalised it in 1983.[2] This merely confirmed its status, along with prostitution, as one of Kalgoorlie's oldest and most important sources of liquid cash.

Football continued to be a great source of entertainment in Kalgoorlie, attracting the patronage of men, women and children. When Dwyer intercepted a crowd returning from a match on 22 September 1907, their mood was so ebullient that they forgot their usual inhibitions about the camera, and smiled, waved and doffed their hats. **(167)**

More sedate games, such as croquet and bowls, also had their followers, but here the numbers were fewer, the clothes formal, and the flags British. **(168)**

By the start of the War, old Kalgoorlie was already changing; and the deaths in conflict of many of its pioneers and their older sons hastened that process of change. **(169)**

---

[2] Danny Sheehan and Wayne Lamotte, *Heads and Tails: The Story of the Kalgoorlie Two-up School* (Grouter Publications, Kalgoorlie, 1985).

A worker takes time off from the construction of a new headframe
and treatment at the Iron Duke to read, 1904

St. Patrick's Day procession, Burt St, Boulder

The headquarters of the Amalgamated Miners' Association

A mass meeting of striking woodcutters, 2 August 1908, addressed by
Julian Stuart, MLA for Leonora

A crowd gathers at Hannan Street to read the results of one of the referenda on conscription

The Executive Council of the Goldfields Reform League, 1900

Laying the foundation stone for the Boulder City Town Hall in December 1907

Ada Crossley breaks convention by going underground at the
Golden Horseshoe gold mine 1904

The Boulder Carnival fair-ground stall of the Rechabites, located behind the Boulder Town Hall

An office of the Mechanics Institute, called a Miners Institute when it opened in 1895,
and used by the local council until 1897

The billiards room (1904-1957) was located in the galvanized iron hall erected at the back of the
Institute in time for the banquet to celebrate the coming of the train in 1896

Miners browse through magazines and newspapers in the Reading Room 1909

Reading on the first-floor verandah of the Institute overlooking Hannan Street 1917

Maurice Geraldo and "The Juggling Geraldos" and others advertised on the
billboard of the Cremorne Gardens 1907

A performance at the new Boulder Town Hall on 23 June 1908

"Hollister Fashion Plates" Fancy Dress Group 1922

A day at Kalgoorlie Race Course in 1914

Flappers and other fashionable types at the Boulder Cup meeting at Boulder Race Course in 1925

Leaving a football match, 22 September 1907

Afternoon shadows fall across a goldfields bowling green c1908

A soldier and the memory of his father 1920

7 OUTSIDERS

170. A studio portrait of the Lanski family, 2 August 1907 (GMM 1025)

171. Orsatti and the Western Australian Sons of Italy, "faithful to their homeland", March 1917 (GMM 1598)

172. Yugoslav Orchestra Hrvatski Tamburasi, Boulder City, 1910

173. Croatian Society (GMM 2078)

174. Mr J. Rafface and family in the studio, 3 September 1907 (GMM 1024)

175. The Battaglia wedding, 20 November 1907 (GMM 1259)

176. Jewish grave of Joseph Salinger, 1907 (GMM 2045)

177. Studio portrait (GMM 2084)

178. Studio portrait with bicycles, 14 October 1907 (GMM 1485)

179. "Coolgardie Pioneers 1894, the girl in white is Miss Kennedy — now Mrs Battie" (A. Reid *Those were the days*, 1933 (1987 R.P.) p. 21.)

180. Aboriginal stockmen taken at racecourse, 1921 (GMM 1959)

181. Hawkines and Aboriginal women (GMM 1328)

182. Prisoner chained to tree at Kurnalpi (GMM 1088)

The outsiders looked different only as Kalgoorlie got older, and more settled in its ways. At the start everyone was an outsider to Western Australia. The 'sandgropers' in fact called the newcomers of the Nineties 't'othersiders', a reference to the predominance of miners from the eastern colonies. When it looked as if the Perth government was not going to join a federated Australia, some goldfielders wanted to secede and form a separate colony, using Esperance as its seaport. Yet, by the 1930s, many of the remaining Kalgoorlie pioneers were now the grey beards urging that Western Australia itself quit the federal system! By then, the young men of the second generation were coming to maturity, and the goldfields' community was a different society. "Those were the days," sighed Arthur Reid in his reminiscences under that title in 1933 and, although the years had mellowed his memories a little, there is no doubt that things had profoundly changed. Old Kalgoorlie could not last forever.

Attitudes to Italians were a litmus test of this change. The Italians were not materially more successful than the rest, but were certainly conspicuous on the goldfields for their high level of mutual co-operation. Co-operation among Italians was essential in this climate of general indifference to their situation; it was also a traditional part of the small-town peasant culture from which they originated. In the northern provinces of Italy, such as Bergamo and Brescia, neighbours were forced to co-operate in order to win a living from the inhospitable environment. The southern Italians who began to flood into the goldfields after the First World War were also accustomed to a fair degree of sharing among family members and 'paesani' generally. What is more, fewer of these new arrivals returned to Italy than the northerners, and the total size of the Italian population in the goldfields grew.

The pioneering generation had been openly dismissive of 'inferior races' such as the Afghans, but became reconciled to the presence of Italians and other southern Europeans in the mining workforce. Generally these men were intinerant bachelors, but occasionally a young family like the Lanskis settled on the goldfields. **(170)**

The southern Europeans organized themselves into social and political clubs and, during the First World War, Italians formed a Sons of Italy chapter. This was also a popular form of organization in the Italian-American settlements, designed principally to advance their commercial interests. The driving force in the Kalgoorlie chapter was Orsatti, but little came of the organization as there were too few permanent Italian residents with an ambition to establish their own small businesses for the idea to work. In their official portrait the Italians declared that they were '*fedeli alla loro patria*' — 'loyal to their homeland', and dressed their mascots in tartans and naval uniforms. **(171)**

Mr Emilio Orsattii found himself in 1919, at the terrifying centre of the first violent outburst against Italians on the goldfields. As licensee of the All Nations Hotel, an old stone and brick building at the lower end of Hannan Street, Orsatti provided a meeting place for itinerant Italian workers, especially those who worked on the Woodline.

Woodline work was hard and poorly rewarded. Each cutter was allocated a block of virgin timber a mile long and two chains wide, which they slowly and single-handedly chopped down, loading the wood in five-or ten-foot lengths on to a cart and trundling back to the main camp. As each area of wood was cut out the whole camp would move a few miles to the next site, laying down rail tracks along the way. The camp had a shanty, where men could drink and sing 'Quel Mazzolin di Fiore', 'Il Cacciatore', 'Se Canta il Mare' and other traditional folk songs.[1] Men and women tended vegetable patches, kept a few pigeons, and otherwise used their peasant skills to survive as comfortably as they could in the circumstances.

In 1919 the Australian Workers' Union organized a strike of the Woodliners to try to lift their wages (they were then cutting from dawn to dusk and getting only about 11/6 per day). Since 800 of the thousand employees were Italian, most of them congregated in Kalgoorlie for the six weeks or so the strike lasted. Hotels such as Orsatti's were natural places to meet, and in August-September, 1919, the striking Italian woodcutters had come in their hundreds.

Unfortunately there were also many unemployed ex-soldiers idle in Kalgoorlie at the same time, and a fight broke out between men from the two groups. A young Italian, Jim (Giacomo) Gatti, stabbed an Anglo-Australian, Thomas Northwood, who died of his wounds several hours later. The following day, after mass meetings and sporadic looting of Italian shops, a crowd of angry miners gathered outside the All Nations. Orsatti and his wife appeared on the balcony and appealed for calm and understanding. As he spoke the crowd broke into the hotel and destroyed its interior. A young Anglo-Australian tried to push Orsatti off the balcony, but the Italian couple were saved by police and led away to safety.

The devastation of Italian hotels and businesses in both Kalgoorlie and Boulder continued, and order was not restored until late in the evening. Orsatti was told by the ex-servicemen's leaders to get the Italians out of town and back on to the Woodlines.

The incident of 1919 was interesting socially as it would be repeated on a grander scale in 1934 when Claudio Mattaboni knocked George Jordan to the pavement, accidentally killing him, and sparked off several days of rioting, looting and physical violence directed at the southern Europeans. The 1919 incident was also interesting industrially, as it was followed by a completely unsuccessful strike the following year. The 1919 strike ended abruptly with the riot, and better, although still inadequate, wages were granted.

In 1920 the ultra-left One Big Union intervened to help the alien workers (just as their counterpart activists did in places like Paterson, New Jersey). This time moderates at the helm of organized labour in Western Australia opposed a strike, and the OBU was defeated.

The newspapers of the day blamed the Italians for being attacked! The logic of the Melbourne *Argus* was as follows:

> *ALIENS IN THE WEST: THE KALGOORLIE ITALIANS: Causes of the Trouble . . . A striking instance of the dangers likely to arise when alien immigrants herd together in little colonies of their own, instead of becoming absorbed in the community, has been given by the events of last week at Kalgoorlie . . . Many of them associate little with the British part of the community, retain their Italian language and habits, and show a fervent, and sometimes aggressive, Italian patriotism, which grows stronger as they get further from Italy. They frequented the wine shops in Kalgoorlie kept by compatriots, and which are closed just now, and under the influence of wine, crowds of Italians would sometimes march down the street singing Italian songs and jostling passers-by . . .*

The newspaper then admitted, without sensing a contradiction, that 'colonies' of Italians in fact lived quite peacefully in various parts of the goldfields: *The trouble has not extended to Leonora and other small places north of Kalgoorlie, at some of which the Italians are said to be in the majority.*[2]

One of these places was Gwalia, where indeed Orsatti had worked before the war as keeper of a boarding house. The Italians dominated the workforce at the Sons of Gwalia mine, living in Gwalia itself rather than the twin town of Leonora. They built themselves simple corrugated-iron houses lined with hessian walls, whitewashed and sometimes tinted with Mediterranean pinks or blues. In the 1920s a local Italian nicknamed 'Angelo Viva' (Michelangelo Incarnate) decorated interiors by daubing a paint-soaked sponge in pleasing designs over the ceilings.

For food, the Italians contrived some local specialities, such as 'little birds and polenta', and the air above Little Italy would crackle with gun-fire as the locals made up for the absence of avifauna in their native land. Those unfortunate galahs, whose flight-path this was, ended up on the table served with the traditional peasant dish, polenta (maize flour and cheese). Goats were also kept by the Italians, and Barney (Bernardo) Mazza

---

[1] L. R. M. Hunter, *Woodline* (The Author, Forrestfield, WA, 1976).

[2] *Argus* (Melbourne) 18 August, 1919, p. 6.

had a recipe calling for 15 goats to every pig used in his famous local sausages.

For diversions the Italians had tug-of-war, jumping, bocce and two-up. Every evening, from the bough sheds behind their houses and the many sly-grog shanties in Gwalia, came the cheerful sounds of Italian singing and music.

Music was a means of communicating with the Anglo-Australians in the goldfields; it was also a way of keeping their spirits up. Some instruments were easy to transport to the other side of the world, especially the Italian piano accordion, long-necked mandolins and various lutes. The result could be the formation of a large ensemble like the Croatian Society string band. **(172, 173)**

Some of the newcomers decided to stay on in Kalgoorlie, and called out their brides and families. They dressed themselves up and asked Dwyer for a photograph, as this was good evidence to send home to assure their 'paesani' that all was going well in the far-off land. **(174, 175)**

Some southern Europeans in fact did very well. Sperandio Battaglia owned a mine at Undamindera. Frank Nazzari arrived on the goldfields in about 1907, worked on the Woodline, and then graduated to ownership of a mine at Ora Banda in the inter-war period. Demetri (Timmy) Frank, a solitary Greek at Burbank, married an Australian-born girl, obtained good tributes, prospered and had four children.

Not many outsiders were buried on the goldfields, as most returned home in their old age. The Jews of Kalgoorlie were few in number; when Joseph Salinger died at the age of 41 in 1907, his wife Rebecca arranged from afar for his burial and headstone. Probably to satisfy his widow that the best possible arrangements had been made for Salinger, Dwyer was commissioned to photograph the grave. **(176)**

The Jewish presence on the goldfields was not significant enough to warrant their own rabbi. When the first Jewish wedding took place in 1897 — between Mr M. L. Cars of the Globe Hotel and Miss Miriam Atherdon — Rabbi Moses Saunders had to make a special trip up from Perth.

All cemeteries are divided up into the different religious groups: Church of England, Methodist, Presbyterian, and Roman Catholic. Nurse Bird remembered the grave-digger MacDougall, who called at the Coolgardie Hospital each morning to obtain estimates of business for the day. He needed the information ahead of time, he explained in his gruff whisper:

'Wull, ye see, nurse, it's this way. The Roman Catholics are fairly easy, for their divusion is all in sand, though it does drubble back as ye dig it. The methody's we can manage weel, too; they go in clay, but it's sticky and a' that, ye ken, no aisy to warrk. But the Churrch of England, they're right on rock, an' I have to blarrst them, an' I must aye be ready. We canna keep the puir bodies waiting for burial, for Coolgardie's vurra warrum! [3]

There was also a category set aside for the rest, including a Japanese grave. The Mazzucelli family, Swiss-Italians, were well-established jewellers in the area, and their deceased, Joseph Antonio, was buried in the Anglican section. In the Catholic section was an Italian, buried under a plain cross with the inscription:

'Erected by Sympathisers in memory of Leo Biretta, Italian Cyclist, aged 23 years, who was killed on the Coolgardie Track, 31st August, 1900.' [4]

There were also Chinese and Japanese residents on the goldfields; they were tolerated, but lived somewhat apart from the majority. Many of the prostitutes at the turn of the century were Japanese women, which may help explain the mood of community acceptance toward the Asian population generally. **(177, 178)**

As the same ex-goldfields' nurse remembered: "*The Japanese were always little gentlemen. Their polish was quite disarming. We wanted to feel angry with them for the way in which most of them made their living in that 'Street of Scarlet Stain'.*"

The dozens of French and Japanese girls who were prostitutes in the early years were victimised by their bosses, or so it was widely believed. As nurse Ann Stafford Bird (later Mrs Garnsey) thought: these girls ' . . . *were such gentle little things, with charming ways; they should have been well cared for and protected by their men, instead of being drugged and used as they were. One little pet of a Japanese — Oyoni — said to me: "I not want get better, nurse. I want go sleep and no more wake up". A few months later she did go to sleep and not wake up.*'[5]

Denis O'Callaghan remembered one incident where some of the most assertive miners decided to take the law into their own hands as far as the foreign prostitutes were concerned:

[3] Ann Stafford Garnsey, *Scarlet Pillows* (Hesperian Press, Perth) pp. 63-64.
[4] *Murdoch University Studies in Industrial Archaeology* 2 (1981) p. 42.
[5] S. Garnsey, *Scarlet Pillows*, pp. 70, 64-65.

Towards the end of May, 1898, a rough mob of undesirables came to the different mining towns. Some of them blew into Kanowna and wrecked a portion of the Japanese women's quarters (women of easy virtue). They smashed windows and doors and fired revolver shots through the galvanised iron walls of the houses. They may have had some provocation, or perhaps did not like the idea of well-dressed Frenchmen (belonging to a syndicate) walking around Kanowna, Kalgoorlie and Coolgardie, in the busy mining centres, with their walking-sticks and gloves, and bludgeoning on poor unfortunate French and Japanese women.[6]

Kalgoorlie could not exist without prostitutes as there were so many single men, some of whom were 'married on the other side and single on this' (referring to the East and West of Australia). For Australian women the occupation of 'singing barmaid' could be pursued with less danger than befell Japanese and French women.

It was not long before business was concentrated in a section of Hannan Street, from where it was transferred to 'the Block' in Hay Street. The origins of this name probably lay in the Victorian capital which so many goldfields had quit in the depressed Nineties. When Melbourne had been 'Marvellous' in the previous decade one of its prized social rituals had been an afternoon promenade up and down 'the Block' (Collins Street between Elizabeth and Swanston Streets). The smartly-dressed lawyers, businessmen and politicians in Melbourne might not have been amused to discover what went on at 'the Block' on the far side of the Nullarbor Plain.

There was one group who lived completely on the margins of Kalgoorlie life: the first inhabitants of the area. Most Aboriginal people stayed in the Bush outside the towns, although some were drawn into certain aspects of European life, showing considerable ability with horses. **(179, 180)**

Black women often had little alternative but to allow Whites to keep them:

In the Widgiemooltha district it is becoming 'the recognised thing' for a prospector to procure a black gin and keep her in his camp . . . And so established has become the custom that more than one instance has occurred where the prospector has sold his camp and his gin to his successor, and the price has been high or low according to the worth and beauty of the "animal". Around Widgiemooltha a black gin is a part of a prospector's camp furniture — a luxury he never attempts to conceal.[7]

Some Europeans, of course, went to great lengths to help the local Aboriginal people, and in so doing became the conscience of the invaders. Everyone in Kalgoorlie knew that the Rev. Canon Collick organised a Christmas feast for the Blacks. Gaunt Aboriginal women, dishevelled and accompanied by pet dogs, were a haunting presence on the streets; they were the leftovers of the original residents. **(181)** In the 1890s organised Aboriginal resistance in Western Australia was crushed with the capture of the Black Ned Kelly, Sandawara.[8]

It was a spirited resistance, but the odds were overwhelming. The diaries of the early prospectors quite candidly reveal the attitudes of the Whites that Aborigines were merely another obstacle to exploration and the discovery of gold. Robert Menzies, who found the 'yellow boy' in the locality of the town named after him, wrote matter-of-factly of his killings:

There they were, natives throwing spears. My boys, crouched behind pack-saddles, were taking a pot-shot at every opportunity . . . We had a merry time for several moments, but bullets own the day. The natives retreated, leaving eight dead". In another encounter, Menzies laid explosives at a water hole: *"Then the fun began. Spears began to come from all sides, then I heard the boom of buried dynamite. Dirt, shrubs and blacks went up into the air. I heard some agonised yells and mad scrambling among the rocks. I threw a few hand-grenades, but no more spears came whizzing about me. I had evidently given them a good scare. At daybreak I walked out to view the 10-minute battle-field. Fourteen dead natives. Blood trails led all over the place, but not a soul was in sight.*[9]

When the battles were done, the Blacks could move further out or become Kalgoorlie fringe-dwellers. In Western Australia white policemen, often assisted by Aboriginal trackers, had extraordinary powers of summary arrest, of chained detention and of remand, in respect of these desert Blacks. **(182)** In Western Australian towns like Kalgoorlie the Aboriginal camps were positioned outside the main settlement, usually alongside the rubbish dump.[10]

[6] Denis O'Callaghan, *Long Life Reminiscences & Adventures Throughout the World* (Shipping Newspapers, Sydney, 1941) p. 250.

[7] 'The groper's slave', *Bulletin* (Sydney) 7 July, 1900, p. 23.

[8] The original white view of Sandawara (Pidgin) was given by Ion Idriess in *Outlaws of the Leopolds* (1952), while the Aboriginal writer Colin Johnson incorporated the story into his urban novel, *Long Live Sandawara* (1979).

[9] Quoted by Philippa Hawker, 'White gold rush, Black pain', *Age* (Melbourne) 2 July, 1984. p 11.

[10] A. O. Neville *Australia's Coloured Minority* (Currawong Publishing, Sydney 1947) pp. 134-135.

The Whites called every Chinese man 'John'; similarly the Blacks called the White man by the generic name 'Bob'. Bob was a capricious master. The very name Kalgoorlie was Bob's best mimickry of the Aboriginal name for the area which is believed to be derived from *Karlkuli*, the Aboriginal word for Silky Pear. When Kalgoorlie was settled by the Whites, the last page in the history of colonial society was turned.

A studio portrait of the Lanski family, 2 August 1907

Orsatti and the Western Australian sons of Italy, "faithful to their homeland", March 1917

Yugoslav Orchestra Hrvatski Tamburasi, Boulder City, 1910

Mr J. Rafface and family in the studio, 3 September 1907

The Battaglia wedding, 20 November 1907

Jewish grave of Joseph Salinger, 1907

Studio portrait

206

Studio portrait with bicycles, 14 October 1907

"Coolgardie Pioneers 1894, the girl in white is Miss Kennedy — now Mrs Battie"

Aboriginal stockmen

Hawkines and Aboriginal women

Prisoner chained to tree at Kurnalpi

ACKNOWLEDGEMENTS

I would like to thank the following people for their assistance with the book — the staff of the Museum of the Goldfields, especially Liz Millward; the staff of Western Australian Museum's Publication department, especially Maureen de la Harpe, Greg Jackson and Ann Ousey; Tom Stannage; David Wood; and my critic, Stuart Macintyre.